Art

Other books in the Careers for the Twenty-First Century series:

Careers
for the
Twenty-First
Century

by Sheri Bell-Rehwoldt

LUCENT BOOKS
An imprint of Thomson Gale, a part of The Thomson Corporation

THOMSON
━━━━✦━━━━ ™
GALE

Detroit • New York • San Francisco • San Diego • New Haven, Conn.
Waterville, Maine • London • Munich

For my husband, Greg.

LIBRARY OF CONGRESS CATALOGING-IN-PUBLICATION DATA

Bell-Rehwoldt, Sheri.
Art / by Sheri Bell-Rehwoldt.
p. cm. — (Careers for the twenty-first century)
Summary: Examines various careers in the arts, including the qualifications, training, and opportunities for each.
Includes bibliographical references and index.
ISBN 1-59018-394-0 (hard cover : alk. paper)
1. Art—Vocational guidance. I. Title. II. Series.
N8350.B45 2004
702'.3'73—dc22
2004010374

Printed in the United States of America

Contents

Foreword

Young people in the twenty-first century are faced with a dizzying array of possibilities for careers as they become adults. However, the advances in technology and a world economy in which events in one nation increasingly affect events in other nations have made the job market extremely competitive. Young people entering the job market today must possess a combination of technological knowledge and an understanding of the cultural and socioeconomic factors that affect the working world. Don Tapscott, internationally known author and consultant on the effects of technology in business, government, and society, supports this idea, saying, "Yes, this country needs more technology graduates, as they fuel the digital economy. But . . . we have an equally strong need for those with a broader [humanities] background who can work in tandem with technical specialists, helping create and manage the [workplace] environment." To succeed in this job market young people today must enter it with a certain amount of specialized knowledge, preparation, and practical experience. In addition, they must possess the drive to update their job skills continually to match rapidly occurring technological, economic, and social changes.

Young people entering the twenty-first-century job market must carefully research and plan the education and training they will need to work in their chosen careers. High school graduates can no longer go straight into a job where they can hope to advance to positions of higher pay, better working conditions, and increased responsibility without first entering a training program, trade school, or college. For example, aircraft mechanics must attend schools that offer Federal Aviation Administration–accredited programs. These programs offer a broad-based curriculum that requires students to demonstrate an understanding of the basic principles of flight, aircraft function, and electronics. Students must also master computer technology used for diagnosing problems and show that they can apply what they learn toward routine maintenance and any number of needed repairs. With further education, an aircraft mechanic can gain increasingly specialized licenses that place him or her in the job market for positions of higher pay and greater responsibility.

In addition to technology skills, young people must understand how to communicate and work effectively with colleagues or clients from diverse backgrounds. James Billington, librarian of Congress, asserts that "we do not have a global village, but rather a globe on which there are a whole lot of new villages . . . each trying to get its own place in the world, and anybody who's going to deal with this world is going to have to relate better to more of it." For example, flight attendants are increasingly being expected to know one or more foreign languages in order for them to better serve the needs of international passengers. Electrical engineers collaborating with a sister company in Russia on a project must be aware of cultural differences that could affect communication between the project members and, ultimately, the success of the project.

The Lucent Books Careers for the Twenty-First Century series discusses how these ideas come into play in such competitive career fields as aeronautics, biotechnology, computer technology, engineering, education, law enforcement, and medicine. Each title in the series discusses from five to seven different careers available in the respective field. The series provides a comprehensive view of what it is like to work in a particular job and what it takes to succeed in it. Each chapter encompasses a career's most recent trends in education and training, job responsibilities, the work environment and conditions, special challenges, earnings, and opportunities for advancement. Primary and secondary source quotes enliven the text. Sidebars expand on issues related to each career, including topics such as gender issues in the workplace, personal stories that demonstrate exceptional on-the-job experiences, and the latest technology and its potential for use in a particular career. Every volume includes an "Organizations to Contact" list as well as annotated bibliographies. Books in this series provide readers with pertinent information for deciding on a career and as a launching point for further research.

Introduction

Art for Life

People who have artistic skill are indeed fortunate. Not only do they possess a talent that is uniquely theirs, but they have a commodity that they can translate into a successful career. Though it is true that an independent artist's fame and fortune is determined in large part by consumer demand, those artists with solid business and marketing skills have a clear advantage over those who do not and are well on their way to gaining commissions and loyal fans. These skills are necessary to give them a competitive edge in the marketplace, as an artist's artistic capabilities will not be appreciated if they are not publicized.

Careers in art are numerous and varied, and many art careers do not require artists to deal with the uncertainties that come with operating their own studios, such as whether they will be able to find clients and sell enough of their work to pay their bills. Art therapists, for example, typically work as part of a hospital staff, while conservators can be found working for museums and corporations whose art objects need to be properly transported, displayed, and stored. Other careers, such as art teacher, graphic designer, and art gallery manager, offer similar job security and benefits. For these people, just working with art, or teaching others about it, is enough to make them feel fulfilled.

The most recent survey from the Research Center for Arts and Culture at Columbia University's Teachers College indicates that the median annual income for an artist is $25,000, with only $5,000 of that derived from actually creating art. Likewise, a recent survey conducted by *U.S. News & World Report* magazine found that 68 percent of artists admitted that they earned less than $20,000 per year for their art—but 73 percent were satisfied with their careers.

Unfortunately, many high school students are advised by family members and school counselors to view their art as a hobby and to pursue more lucrative careers instead, such as law, medicine, or business. Students who have the courage—and the talent—to follow their dreams may be pleasantly surprised at how well their art careers work out. But to find success, students

There are many career paths open to artists, like this landscape painter, who wish to market their artistic talents.

will have to be dedicated to perfecting their craft and willing to work for years to build a flourishing business. Persistence, and an unwavering belief in their talent, is the key.

As so many in the field already know, a career in art is a tantalizing choice. Although there are big unknowns, art-related careers can offer individuals the opportunity to explore and refine their artistic vision. The good news is that true artistic skill has long been rewarded, and it can be expected to be even more so as our society becomes increasingly visual.

Chapter 1

Conservators

The job of an art conservator is to preserve cultural property, whether found in a museum, in a private lab, or even in a collection held by a private corporation. Cultural property may include paintings, documents, photographs, textiles, architectural structures, or objects such as vases, ceremonial masks, or sculpture. Art conservators work to ensure that these objects stay intact for future generations to enjoy. They do this by carefully cleaning, treating, and monitoring the works and suggesting appropriate housing and display of the objects, which can be made from paper, animal skin, canvas, wood, fiber, film, or stone. Most conservators specialize in one area, such as treating objects fashioned from paper. A paper conservator might handle the Declaration of Independence, old letters from famous authors, or artwork drawn or painted on heavy card stock.

Why Conservation Is Necessary

Just as human health is affected by diet and exposure to the elements, art objects are at the mercy of their environments. Art conservators work to prevent—and stall—deterioration that naturally occurs due to light levels, pollution, chemicals, and mishandling. A painting, for instance, may develop cracks if placed in a room that has a fluctuating temperature. Likewise, high humidity levels can invite mold; too little moisture, on the other hand, may cause some objects to disintegrate. Bug infestation is another threat. Through intensive graduate-level training and on-the-job learning, a conservator is able to deal with all of these scenarios.

Conservators may be hired as staff members at museums or corporations, but many choose to work independently, going into business for themselves. Ellen Riggs Tillapaugh, a paper conservator who works from her home lab in Cooperstown, New York, handles restoration projects for private clients and for museums, regional art centers, and historical societies that do not have the budgets to hire staff conservators. With her training and experience, Tillapaugh is often able to reverse the damage inflicted on works of art. However, one of her most important duties is to prevent that damage by advising her clients on proper storage and display techniques. She explains:

> I can treat a print or watercolor, clean it to remove stains or discolorations, and have it look very pristine. But if the

An Italian conservator cleans and restores the arms of a sculpture. Conservators protect art objects from deterioration.

owner hangs that artwork in bright sunlight, or on a wall with southern exposure, there will be fading of the media. Once ink or watercolor fades, it can never be brought back; it is permanent damage. So, providing guidance to the owner on the care of the artwork becomes the most important "treatment care" I can provide.[1]

Important as this work is, few people outside the art world have heard of the art conservator. But awareness of this field is growing, thanks in part to some high-profile projects such as the cleaning of the Statue of Liberty and of Auguste Rodin's world-famous sculpture *The Thinker*. In addition, television programs such as *This Old House* and *Antiques Roadshow* have reminded viewers that items from the past can have significant monetary value—in addition to their sentimental value—if properly cared for. Unfortunately, many people have a negative effect on this value because they are unaware of the object's history or how the item should be handled. According to the American Institute for Conservation of Historic and Artistic Works (AIC),

> We live in an era of fascination with mementos of the past. Countless television viewers tune in faithfully to popular programs such as *The Antiques Roadshow* to enjoy the vicarious thrill of learning that a grandparent's painting, stored for years in the attic, is an important work of folk art, or that a much-loved doll has become a valuable antique. Just as often, however, observers have sympathized with the unfortunate folks who unknowingly destroyed the value of a brass lamp or a bronze medal by polishing away the original patina. Such disappointments underscore the need for clear and understandable information on how to care for beloved family treasures.[2]

A Conservator's Role

In part, the job of an art conservator is not well-known because of the nature of the work. Conservators work behind the scenes. As Jonathan Thornton, a professor of objects conservation at Buffalo State College, says, "What conservators essentially do is invisible; what we do to artwork is not supposed to be seen."[3]

Conservators approach each piece of art in need of repair with caution and respect. They can spend many hours just researching the age, function, and construction of a piece so that they understand how best to treat it. Only when they are sure of the cause and severity of damage do the conservators spend time contemplating which techniques and materials they can use to repair or stabilize the object. As conservation has solidified in only the last fifty years, there is still much to learn about appropriate techniques and materials.

Art conservators apply their artistic and problem-solving skills to every damaged art object using a guiding principle called "reversibility." This means that they strive to use only techniques and products that will not damage an object, and those that can easily and safely be separated from the object as needed. An art conservator would carefully determine which resins, bleaches, pigments, and protective coatings might work best and would not, for example, use a tape recognized to be detrimental to paper when repairing a tear on a manuscript. Nor would a conservator use a solvent known to react with glue or to cause discoloring if he or she were repairing a shattered white or clear-glass vase.

As well, art conservators certainly would not brighten the hue of a garment in an oil painting or decide to paint in a horse just because they thought it made the painting somehow look better. That is not their job. Instead, an art conservator's role is to stabilize an object's condition and determine how best to prevent further or future damage.

To advance knowledge within the field, conservators around the world freely share treatment choices with one another. And keeping the possibility of future repairs of the object in mind, conservators carefully document how they conserved the item so that future conservators can understand why they chose particular treatment options. The written records explain the problem, the solution, and any concerns the conservator may have had. Conservator Joan Gardner explains the process she and other conservators in her museum use when restoring an item from the museum's collection:

We take photographs of it before we work on it, during the time we work on it, and then after we're finished. What we

A conservator restores a painted ceiling in an Italian church. Because art restoration is such delicate and precise work, conservators must undergo years of formalized training.

are really trying to do is document what an object's made of, what we used on it, and why we did it, so there's a record for history. We're record keepers as well as people who intervene.[4]

Preparing to Be a Conservator

Conservators undergo years of formalized training before they are given the opportunity to independently handle objects. Since the field is small, competition for jobs is tough; training and experience often determine who is considered for an opening. Even just twenty years ago, if someone wanted to become a conservator, he or she most likely applied to a museum and learned the skills on the job. This is no longer the case.

Students now considering a career in conservation need graduate-level training from one of the handful of universities in the United States offering graduate conservation programs, including Buffalo State College, the University of Delaware, New York University, and the University of Texas at Austin. But first they must secure undergraduate degrees, typically in art, chemistry, or art history. Conservation is very much based on the understanding of how solutions and materials interact, so students must demonstrate their comprehension of organic chemistry. Jae Mentzer, a third-year student at the University of Delaware, says many people talk themselves out of a career in conservation because they become intimidated by these science requirements. She urges students not to do this, explaining that persistence can turn that fear into a determination to succeed: "Chemistry is crucial, but if you really want to go into conservation, you can do it. I have one classmate who majored as an undergrad in chemistry, and another in biochemistry. But there are others who were anthropology majors and art history majors."[5]

While acquiring their undergraduate degrees, many students take advantage of museum-studies classes and conservation-based work-study positions to prepare for admission to graduate programs. Even working in a museum's administrative office can be helpful in exposing them to the various issues affecting the physical safety of museum collections. Sally Malenka, a conservator of sculpture and decorative arts at the Philadelphia Museum of Art, describes the path she took to become a conservator:

> My undergraduate degree was in anthropology. I was working at the Smithsonian's Museum of Natural History. I liked the work the conservators were doing and decided to go into conservation. There were many college classes I had to take first, including studio arts and science classes. And I began volunteering in the conservation lab to acquire skills.[6]

A Portfolio Is the Key

Taking the required undergraduate classes is only the first step in getting accepted into a university's graduate conservation program.

Each school typically accepts only ten students per year to keep lab sizes small, so competition for the slots is fierce. Candidates are chosen based on their commitment to professional conservation practices and their familiarity with art and science. They also need hand skills, or dexterity, to put that knowledge into practice.

A well-rounded art portfolio is perhaps the most critical factor in gaining acceptance into a graduate program. A candidate's portfolio must demonstrate artistic technique, but not necessarily an abundance of artistic creativity. Thornton shares what he looks for in the portfolio of a person applying to the three-year graduate program at Buffalo State College:

> We're looking for skill, but not necessarily talent; someone who can do careful work in a variety of media. We want them to have good knowledge and sensitivity to art, but they don't need to have artistic talent. What we're after is the ability to draw, the ability to do a nice copy of someone else's work. It's really copy versus creativity. This is the reason many people state for going into conservation. They love to draw, but didn't feel they had the creativity for the gallery life, which requires a strong ego.[7]

During the interview and selection process, students are asked to prove their artistic knowledge and skill and their effectiveness in communicating and problem solving. Mentzer recalls her interview process at the University of Delaware:

> There was a writing test, a still-life drawing test, and a color-vision test. I was given twenty minutes to present slides that demonstrated my experience in conservation, which I talked about while my portfolio was circulating. They asked me to explain why I did things, looking for problem-solving skills. And I had to choose an art object from a table of objects. The faculty asked me questions about the object, such as "What do you think its function was?" "How old do you think it is?" and "How would you display this object?" They were looking for me to demonstrate a sense of history. My instructors talk a lot about the "three-legged stool." By this, they mean that conservators

King Kamehameha's Face-Lift

King Kamehameha I, who died in 1819, is famous for unifying the Hawaiian Islands. Each year, local residents celebrate Kamehameha Day on June 11 to commemorate his achievement. Students, enjoying the reprieve from school, join in the festivities, which include a parade and the presenting of leis to large statues of the king. The first casting of the statue, which was for a time lost at sea, now stands watch over the town of Napa'au in North Kohala, the king's birthplace, on the Big Island of Hawaii.

In preparation for the parade in 1996, conservator Glenn Wharton assessed the sculpture and discovered that, over a number of years, the statue's original detailing had been covered over with twenty-five layers of paint. To allow the statue to appear as its artist intended, Wharton stripped the layers with pressurized water. In doing so, he discovered that the statue had previously undetected feathers on its costuming. Happy that the statue had been returned to its original condition, the local citizens asked Wharton to train them in conducting routine maintenance so they could ensure that the statue retained its refreshed appearance.

In 1996 conservator Glenn Wharton restored Hawaii's statue of King Kamehameha I to its original appearance.

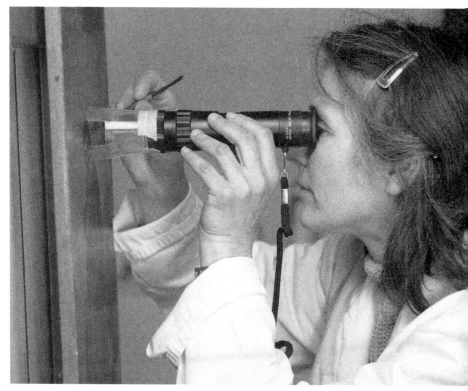

A conservator uses an illuminated magnifying glass to help restore a painting. Conservators learn such specialized techniques of restoration in postgraduate study.

must have good hand skills, a strong understanding of chemistry, and a historical/art-historical background.[8]

Benefits of Graduate Training

Once a student is accepted into a graduate training program, he or she usually completes two or three years of coursework and a one-year internship in a museum setting. Students immerse themselves in the histories of art and conservation, archaeology, materials science, and treatment techniques. In their second year of training, students choose a specialty, such as paintings, sculpture, decorative arts, textiles, archival and library materials, or electronic media. The training is intensive, as the students must learn the history of their art objects and the materials and techniques used in conserving them. Students can choose to develop more than one specialty, but typically no more than two, to ensure that they are able to focus on becoming experts in those areas.

Thornton says it is not uncommon for students to enter the program thinking they want to work in one area but then deciding to take a different route in the middle of their training. Students are exposed to a variety of projects so that they can determine which area of conservation most satisfies them. Thornton describes the range of art objects his students at Buffalo State College might handle during their training: "Yesterday they worked on a variety of things, including American Indian baskets, beaded moccasins, African sculpture, an eighteenth-century globe, a modern fiberglass sculpture, archaeological finds, and Egyptian mummy coverings."[9]

Many conservation graduates opt to extend their training by applying for postgraduate fellowship positions in museum settings. Doing so can be a smart way to get a foot in the door at a museum that is not currently hiring. Conservators who work in fellowships, funded by foundations such as the Andrew W. Mellon Foundation and the J. Paul Getty Trust, are referred to as "fellows." Malenka describes what the career path might be for a conservator who is nearing the completion of a fellowship: "A fellow might apply for a job as an assistant conservator, then maybe four or five years later for a job as an associate conservator. Each step has a portfolio attached to it. Advancement may be affected by the number of staff and the resources of the museum."[10]

Safety in the Workplace

Before anyone can work in the field, whether as a fellow or a professional conservator, they must learn how to safely use and store chemicals. Art conservators may handle any number of chemicals or solvents as they work on various objects. Some of these solvents can cause explosions if stored or handled incorrectly. Because of these dangers, conservators are required to follow government guidelines that outline how to label, store, and dispose of these hazardous wastes. While a self-employed conservator might handle this herself, a large museum might assign one staff person to oversee these details for the entire conservation department. Because breathing in these chemicals can lead to respiratory problems and lung disease, conservators are required to use respirators to protect themselves. If a lab is not using proper safety practices, it is most certainly putting the health of its workers at risk. Mentzer recalls how her graduate instructors stressed the importance of working only in safe environments:

> We were trained how to take chemicals from the storeroom properly, how to dispose of them, and the importance of working with proper ventilation. In my first year I was fitted

Important Health and Safety Precautions

Although conservation is an exciting and rewarding career, Monoa Rossol, an industrial hygienist who specializes in the dangers of the hazardous chemicals used in art careers, cautions that conservators must be aware of the health risks, such as respiratory problems, associated with the handling, storing, and disposing of hazardous materials. Some of these materials include pigments, preservatives, and cleaning chemicals.

Pigments, which are used on historic artworks, are dangerous because they usually contain toxic substances, including arsenic, lead, mercury, cadmium, manganese, and cobalt. Unfortunately, the pigments often flake off objects as conservators handle and repair them.

Preservatives can also be found lingering on old art objects, because they were heavily used in the past by conservators. Many of the preservatives include compounds of arsenic and mercury and banned pesticides such as DDT, which are hazardous even in small amounts.

In addition, some cleaning chemicals are highly flammable and toxic, and others are corrosive acids. Using and storing these materials can be dangerous, particularly because some of them can start fires if accidentally mixed. And certain chemicals, such as ethyl ether and picric acid, cannot be kept too long or they can explode with the force of TNT.

To address these dangers, conservators routinely wear protective equipment such as gloves, eyewear, and respirators. They also install fume hoods to vent the hazardous gases out of their labs.

with a respirator. I was taught how to change the cartridges. You don't want to be cavalier about solvents, even though you're using a very small amount; you have to consider the long-term effect over the years.[11]

To provide further protection from exposure to toxic gases and dust, labs make use of fume hoods. A fume hood is perhaps a lab's most important piece of safety equipment. It vents gases to the outside of a building and protects the art conservator working with chemicals from possible fires and explosions.

The design of a lab is also important. A quality lab offers a variety of work areas for simultaneous projects; a microscope and dental lamp for looking at fibers and paint layers; and a variety of tools such as brushes, spatulas, adhesives, and scalpels. Karen Pavelka, a university library paper conservator, describes the ideal lab as one that is "clean and well organized. There's a formality to a lab setting. You don't eat there, and you don't let the public wander in the lab unattended."[12]

The Thrill of New Challenges

Conservation graduates soon find that, unlike in other careers, there is no typical workday for an art conservator. For example, Tillapaugh might spend one week conducting a general conservation survey for a museum, reviewing the collection's light levels, temperature, humidity, ventilation, air quality, and storage facilities, while the next week she might be meeting with potential clients about conserving a paper-based item they discovered in an attic. Thornton adds that he enjoys the unpredictability conservation offers: "The work is always different, and that's both terrifying and rewarding. We get to work very closely with things that other people don't get to touch. I'm working with beautiful, wonderful things. It's a privilege."[13]

Travel is another exciting aspect of conservation. In her role as a paper conservator and lecturer, Pavelka has worked with conservators from around the world, and has traveled to Argentina, London, and Spain. She shares some of her on-the-job activities:

I have one of the most diverse jobs I can imagine. I get to do conservations . . . and spend a lot of time looking into the histories of documents. Also, I've been an expert witness,

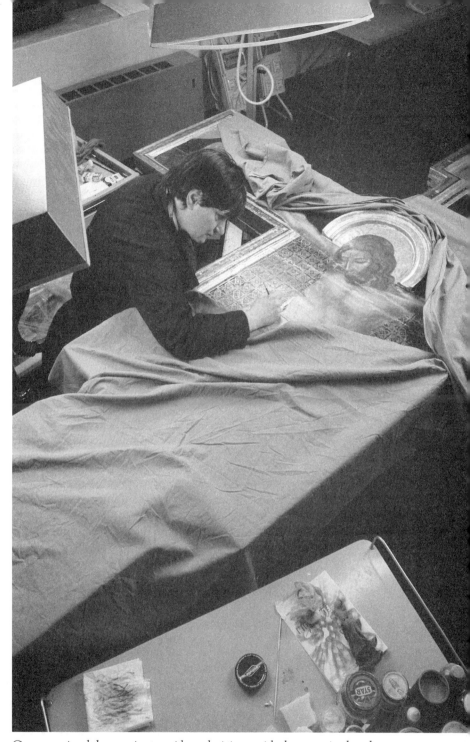

Conservation laboratories provide technicians with the organized and properly ventilated work environment they need. Here, an Italian conservator works on a crucifixion scene.

testifying whether an ink would have been used in a certain time period. One of my most challenging projects was conserving an early John Milton document. [John Milton was an English poet in the 1600s.] It was a Greek and Latin lesson from when he was a student at Oxford. It had been previously repaired with really heavy strips of paper along the edges. And someone had repaired one of the tears with a piece of vellum tape. I had to dissolve the vellum working under a microscope with an enzyme, fiber by fiber. It took me six hours to get it off. The entire project took me 125 hours.[14]

Who Makes a Good Conservator?

While a conservator need not have the artistic skills of Michelangelo, there are some needed traits that those in the field say are critical. An art conservator must have good hand skills for handling precise work, as well as healthy eyes and good color

Conservators often make creative decisions in order to protect artwork. Here, conservators at the Louvre in Paris decided to secure paintings in crates in anticipation of flooding in 2003.

vision, which is why graduate programs require eye exams as part of their interview process. An art conservator must also possess patience and the ability to concentrate. Pavelka explains this: "You have to have the personality to become captivated by something. Try taking a piece of paper and staring at it for two minutes. Your eye will start to pick up more and more detail. You also need nerves of steel, because your obligation is to the artifact. You have to learn to handle a situation without panicking. For instance, if a work starts to 'bleed,' you have to be able to focus on that 100 percent."[15]

An art conservator is curious, resourceful, able to make creative treatment decisions, and able to work in isolation as necessary. However, he or she also has to work well in a team environment. Sometimes restoration decisions are determined by a senior conservator and then carried out by junior conservators, or treatment plans are made through group consensus, with members of the conservation team handling different aspects of the restoration. Being able to articulately engage in dialogue, accept feedback, and listen to other viewpoints are critical skills when working in a museum or corporation setting. Thornton shares why good interpersonal and communication skills are so important for a conservator to develop: "A lot of conservators are not comfortable being 'front people,' but people skills are highly valued. You have to be able to talk to curators and collections-care managers and work smoothly with them. You need to talk well and present your positions well."[16]

Lastly, conservators possess a high sense of professional ethics and do not abuse their artistic powers. This means that they stay focused on doing only what is best for a piece of art because of the responsibility they feel to the creator of the object. They do not think that the art object becomes theirs just because they are restoring it. In actuality, they are playing only a small role in the object's history. This is why people go into conservation. They love art and gain immense satisfaction in knowing that their efforts ensure that future generations will have the opportunity to view the art objects.

Earnings and Opportunities

Art conservators find work in museums, regional centers, private companies, independent labs, and even archaeological digs. Those

Caring for Books

Conservators often teach their private clients how to properly handle, shelve, and store book collections to ensure that they will remain in good condition. Because they are made of paper, which is particularly susceptible to environmental influences such as light, temperature, and humidity, books must be treated with care.

Although a home library's incandescent lights are less harmful than the fluorescent lights found in many libraries and offices, conservators still stress that lights should be turned off when rooms are not in use, and that bright sunlight be blocked by curtains, shades, or plastic filtering films.

Extreme temperatures also damage books. Heat makes leather covers brittle, while damp conditions encourage mold to grow. Conservators recommend that books should be kept away from heat sources, including radiators and fireplaces, and air-conditioning programmed to keep room temperature at a steady 70 degrees to prevent damage.

How books are shelved is also important. They should stand vertically on bookshelves, supported by bookends. Books should not be packed too tightly or they might be damaged as they are removed. Good air circulation is crucial.

Everyday handling of books also inflicts damage, due to the dirt and oil from fingertips. Conservators recommend that old books be handled only when white gloves are worn. Dropping books is bad for them as well, as is putting stress on a book's spine if it is placed flat open on a surface. Even photocopying a book is detrimental unless the copier allows the user to keep the book at a 90-degree angle to reduce stress.

Conservators are quick to point out all of these tips, as they know that if handled with care, book collections can last for many years.

choosing to set up independent conservation businesses usually attach workshops to their homes. As work environments vary significantly, salaries for art conservators also vary. Recent graduates from conservation programs typically make no more than

$30,000 per year. Conservators with five years of experience might earn $40,000 to $60,000 per year, while more senior conservators, or those in administrative roles, may earn more than $100,000 per year.

Because the conservation field is competitive, with a slow turnover rate, getting that first job is a challenge. Art conservators with a graduate degree and ample volunteer and paid experience have the best chance when applying for positions. Freelancing offers conservators the most flexibility in working on projects they like, but those choosing this route need considerable business skills and connections within the industry in order to find clients. Marketing and promotion skills are also important, as is having the finances needed to purchase a wide range of lab equipment and chemicals, as well as insurance. Teaching is another option, though these jobs are scarce and require significant experience. Administrative positions in museums are more attainable, but many conservators prefer jobs that allow them to continue their hands-on project work.

On the whole, art conservators enjoy a wide range of activities, as well as stimulating interaction. They often collaborate with professionals from related fields, such as computer science, museum curatorship, exhibit design, archival studies, and digital imaging to ensure the successful preservation and conservation of an art object. But no matter how they interact or with whom, conservators produce results. This career challenges people, allows them to surround themselves daily with art, and gives them an immense sense of satisfaction. Pavelka says art conservation is the career of a lifetime: "Conservation allows you to work with really cool stuff. The best is knowing that you're doing something to further the life of the cultural heritage. It's my job to make sure that everything in the library lasts as long as it is needed. That's fun and challenging."[17]

Chapter 2

Jewelry Designers

Jewelry designers are part artisan and part technician. They have an appreciation of what looks visually appealing but also are skilled in translating design ideas into wearable art using a variety of techniques, such as enameling and silversmithing. In doing so they might incorporate precious gems, metals, textiles, stones, or everyday objects such as buttons, photos, or watch parts to create pieces of wit, whimsy, or breathtaking beauty.

Jewelry designers relish working with their hands, expressing their own creative flair as they create miniature works of art that others choose to adorn themselves with. Designer and instructor Carles Codina sums up the appeal this way: "In a rational and demanding society where the relationship between an activity and its outcome is felt less and less, manual labor, and ultimately the creative process, allows one to create a tiny object that can then be shown off, put on, or given away—thereby both revealing and understanding one's self a little better."[18]

From the big-city showrooms of celebrity designers such as Tiffany's to the summer-long street festivals where local designers sell their pieces, jewelry designers have many opportunities to display and sell their work. If jewelry designers are able to successfully market their skill, they can enjoy lucrative and fulfilling careers. Established designers, often employing large staffs to fashion their art, can command substantial sales just on their reputations.

To position themselves for financial success, new designers spend considerable time developing strong business skills. They learn accounting skills, including how to set prices that more than cover their costs, and marketing skills such as how to effectively share their design knowledge with potential buyers. As well, designers develop strong work habits, such as focus, discipline, flexibility, patience, and reliability. These are necessary because if designers cannot meet deadlines for delivering inventory to clients, for example, they will not remain in business.

Avenues of Education

Most important, however, are a designer's artistic abilities. This is not an industry that demands specific training, so many designers

Jewelry designers must have both an artistic eye and the technical skills needed to transform design ideas into wearable art. Here, a woman makes porcelain buttons and brooches.

learn through trial and error, on their own, or from books. Others choose to learn in a classroom environment. Some designers obtain a bachelor of fine arts (BFA) or master of fine arts (MFA) degree from a college or university, while others attend a formal trade school or invest in short, intense workshops at craft centers and schools that focus on a single process or technique they want to master.

Artists like this woman creating gold jewelry learn the delicate art of jewelry making through trial and error, through independent study, or by attending school.

Students can begin developing their design skills early. Middle and high school art or shop classes are ideal, as are youth art classes offered by local museums and art centers. Some high school students may even have access to local college programs that offer introductory courses in jewelry design. The Maryland Institute College of Art (MICA) in Baltimore, for instance, features a fourteen-week course titled "Introduction to Art Jewelry." The course is part of MICA's Portfolio Prep program for high school juniors and seniors who need to prepare an art portfolio for entry into an art or design program. The admission committees of these programs use the portfolios to determine which students have budding artistic ability. The MICA jewelry course gives students a head start in creating pieces, introducing them to the technical skills they need to begin making their own jewelry. The weekly sessions teach skills in sawing, soldering, polishing, riveting, surface embellishment, and forming.

For those students who want to earn a BFA for their design skills, there are approximately 180 college and university programs across the country that offer jewelry design programs. They also give students the credentials they need to teach after they graduate or to continue on to an MFA program. Two schools with fine BFA program reputations are the East Carolina University School of Art, located in Greenville, North Carolina, and the Tyler School of Art in Elkins Park, Pennsylvania.

The Craft School Route

For students unwilling or unable to commit four years to an academic degree, a number of prestigious craft schools throughout the United States offer hands-on training in jewelry design and manufacturing. Students can attend workshops in blacksmithing, ceramics, fibers, glass, graphics, metals, or woodworking.

The Penland School of Crafts, for example, in the Blue Ridge Mountains of North Carolina offers intensive one- and two-week workshops on paper, clay, drawing, glass, iron, metals, photography, printmaking, textiles, and wood to both the novice and experienced designer. The sessions are taught by experts from around the country who are commercially successful. More than twelve hundred people attend workshops at Penland each year. Instruction is open to anyone with interest who is at least eighteen years of age.

The cost of individual workshops can run several thousand dollars but include housing, meals, educational slide shows, and round-the-clock access to the design studios, which students in university programs do not have. The craft schools keep their studios open so that students have the time and tools to perfect their new skills before returning to their home studios.

Maggi DeBaecke, a jewelry designer living in Pennsylvania, frequently participates in Penland workshops. She believes that the access to the studio, and the collaborative atmosphere generated by the participants' high energy and enthusiasm, allows students to learn at a faster pace than is possible in university programs. She adds that some designers are better suited to the less-rigid environment: "If you have a student who's not doing well academically but is highly creative, I highly recommend he or she go to a crafts school. In two weeks they'll learn a whole semester of jewelry making because the teachers are at the top of their fields and the studios are always open."[19]

Like DeBaecke, Delaware jewelry designer Maxine Rosenthal continues to develop her skills through hands-on instruction. To supplement her knowledge gained from several semesters of jewelry design at the University of Delaware, Rosenthal takes two or three workshops a year at colleges, art centers, and design guilds to hone her technique. Even after designing jewelry for thirteen years, Rosenthal appreciates the value of these classes and says they are particularly beneficial to new designers trying to figure out what areas of design interest them.

Design Style

Some designers take the arts and crafts route, choosing to sell relatively inexpensive jewelry to the general public at festivals, crafts shows, and other events. They mass-produce a number of similar items that they can sell relatively inexpensively to simultaneous outlets. Buyers interested in the latest fashion craze are filling the bank accounts of these designers. For instance, hordes of teens have purchased the mood ring, which changes color according to body heat, since the 1970s.

Other jewelry designers find they are drawn to creating high-end, one-of-a-kind pieces. As a result, they sell to a smaller clientele who can afford their use of costly jewels and metals. In addition, displaying and selling these expensive pieces requires that these designers choose venues that offer substantial security, such as heavily guarded shops and galleries.

Though a new designer might want to create only one-of-a-kind pieces, Rosenthal says that new designers most likely will not have the financial freedom to do so. It takes time to build a design business and gain a following, and most people cannot afford to collect expensive jewelry. Rosenthal says that the reality is that "if you decide you're going to support yourself solely with your own work, you probably have to supplement it with some production work or teaching."[20]

Publicity

The key to design independence is building a reputation. Designers do this through publicity. Heidi Kummli, a self-taught jewelry designer, says she has been able to focus on fashioning her intricate one-of-a-kind bead pieces, which take significant time to create, because of the publicity she has received from winning design competitions. She suggests that jewelry designers enter as many competitions as possible—and early in their careers—for

A designer displays pieces for sale at a jewelry fair in Indonesia. Designers who create expensive jewelry prefer such venues because they offer substantial security.

the exposure they provide. In 2003 Kummli took first place in the bead category of the prestigious Saul Bell Design Award competition, which recognizes innovative, quality design. The publicity from the competition helped to establish Kummli's niche in beadwork. She won the category with "Nature's Jewels," an elaborate bead embroidery necklace with bead fringe, which took her more than two years to complete in her spare time. The piece, based on Kummli's effort to reproduce the feathers of a hummingbird, incorporates multicolored beads, cabochon (a gemstone cut so as to have a domed surface on one side and a flat surface on the other), and fancy-cut gemstones stitched to an ultra-suede backing. As a result of industry press, and her promotion of herself through her Web site, Kummli's jewelry is now purchased by avid collectors all over the world.

Jewelry designers can also garner publicity from entering and winning local and national art grants. Though it takes considerable time to adequately fill out the required paperwork and write

Mimicking the Masters

For many designers who enjoy replicating jewelry from early civilizations, surviving Egyptian artifacts offer an endless fount of inspiration. Egyptians wore jewelry for many reasons, including protecting themselves against bad omens. Modern designers have borrowed numerous design elements from Egyptian amulets, collars, earrings, breastplates, diadems, rings, necklaces, anklets, and hair ornaments. Their contemporary designs are often inlaid with the same materials the Egyptians favored, such as gold, silver, copper, lapis lazuli, turquoise, and other semiprecious materials as well as stones, shells, minerals, metals, and the bones from animals, birds, and fish. The Egyptians also favored particular color schemes, which modern designers have been quick to appreciate, such as the color red, which the Egyptians believed symbolized energy and power. Contemporary designers also often use the semiprecious jewels the Egyptians first stylized, including turquoise, serpentine, green jasper, and peridot.

the artist's statement, which asks the designer to share his or her design philosophies and techniques in at least a paragraph, Rosenthal says that there are some benefits to the lengthy admission process: "It's like a lot of other things in life: You wonder if it's worth all the trouble. But while you're doing so, you learn lots of skills that you will use in marketing your work. Having to write an artist statement made me much more comfortable talking about my work."[21]

Another option for jewelry designers to build publicity is to develop long-term relationships with galleries and stores, which may eventually display their pieces. Gallery owners like Ivan Barnett, who opened the Patina Gallery in Sante Fe, New Mexico, appreciates one-of-a-kind jewelry, as well as museum-quality ceramic sculpture and textile art. Barnett explains how he decides which designers to carry:

> We travel the country looking for talented artists who are making pieces that are totally different from everyone else's. We also look at dozens of portfolios that artists send us for review. We look at all aspects of what each person is doing; we are interested in the whole artists, not just their latest works. That means a commitment to the long term is key. Most of our artists have been making jewelry for at least 15 years.[22]

Retail Shows

Small, independent jewelry designers, lacking the marketing dollars and staffs that larger design houses enjoy, have to work hard to catch the eye of galleries and clients. Less-established designers cannot afford expensive advertising, such as the large glossy ads in a Sunday newspaper, so they have to attract clients in other ways. Designers typically spend at least 20 percent of their time marketing themselves, gaining a following in their communities by teaching classes, offering pieces of their jewelry for charity auctions, and speaking at local events. Those ready to expand beyond their local area often do so via the Internet and by attending retail and wholesale shows.

Retail shows invite the general public to peruse the work of numerous artists, whereas wholesale shows permit only retailers—such as shop owners and buyers for well-known store

A potential client examines a pair of earrings at a retail show. Independent designers often show their work at such events in order to attract buyers.

chains—who place large orders that will be resold at higher prices to the public. Designers participating in retail shows arrive with ample inventory to sell. Whatever inventory remains unsold is taken to their next show. If a designer sells out of all of her earrings, or a particular necklace that she knows is a big seller, she will have to hurry back to the studio to create those pieces—or direct her staff to do so and ship them—in time for her next show. Because designers cannot know what will sell out, they tend to stagger their attendance at retail shows to give themselves time to replenish their stock.

Some of the most prestigious retail shows include the Washington Craft Show, the Smithsonian Craft Show, and the Philadelphia Museum of Art Craft Show. Thousands of people visit these shows, which are typically held over a weekend, for the thrill of viewing the work of the best artisans in the country. The rental fees for booths, paid by the jewelry designers and other show vendors, go toward some artistic endeavor. Funds raised from the Philadelphia Museum of Art show, for example, are tapped to purchase works of art, to fund conservation and publication projects, and to support exhibitions and education programs.

All three prestigious shows are highly competitive, juried shows. This means that jewelry designers who wish to participate—and get in on the publicity both before and during the show—must compete for the privilege of being one of the featured vendors. Before the show, the artists submit slides of their work, which each show's jurors evaluate for technical skill, quality of workmanship, and originality of design. Being accepted into a show is difficult unless an artist uncovers the unwritten requirements. For example, pictures should be large enough for judges to see the details but not so large that they appear unprofessional. Rosenthal recounts her first attempts:

> I was told to submit slides that were a good representation of my work, so I took a representative sample of pieces to a professional photographer. But my first three applications were rejected. I determined that there might be other rules that I didn't know about. An experienced friend taught me the real rules of the game are that, one, you present a consistent body of work that shows maturity, which means that the pieces should relate to each other; two, the pieces you choose should be your very best ones; and three, your work should take up three-fourths of the slide. I redid my slides and suddenly I started getting into shows.[23]

Wholesale Shows

While retail shows bring in crowds of people eager to look at—and perhaps buy—jewelry, some artists admit that they find the mobs of people too intimidating. These designers are better suited to the pace of wholesale shows. At such shows, designers deal

A Peek at the British Monarchy's Crown Jewels

The British Crown Jewels are famous worldwide as a symbol of the monarchy. In use by British kings and queens for centuries, their historical value is incalculable. As they are some of the world's most perfect stones, they also have astronomical financial value.

Among the jewels are the Cullinan I (or the Great Star of Africa), a pear-shaped diamond mounted in the head of the Royal Scepter. At 530.2 carats, it is considered to be the world's largest cut diamond. A carat is a measurement used by those in the jewelry business, and is equal to 200 milligrams. Weights are given to the nearest 1/100 of a carat, an amount that is called a point. A 0.50 carat gemstone might also be called one-half carat or a 50-point stone.

The Cullinan II (or Lesser Star of Africa), weighing in at 317.4 carats, is the showpiece of the Imperial State Crown. The diamond, the world's second-largest cut diamond, has two tiny platinum loops along its edges so that it can be worn alone as a brooch or be combined with the Cullinan I. Both diamonds are part of the Cullinan Diamond, which was found in South Africa in 1905. It was the largest rough, gem-quality diamond ever found, at 3,106 carats. Queen Elizabeth also has a brooch that includes two other stones cut from the Cullinan Diamond. Separately they

weigh 94.4 and 63.6 carats. Collectively, the British Crown Jewels are some of the world's most valuable and beautiful pieces.

The Imperial State Crown contains some of the world's most perfect stones.

The hazards of working with jewelry include eyestrain and exposure to toxic chemicals. Here, employees at a jewelry company make pieces in a properly lighted and ventilated facility.

with a handful of store buyers—who may put in orders for one hundred of the same piece. The benefit of the larger sales means that the designers will not have to attend as many shows as does a designer participating in retail shows. They will not be on the road as much, but they face a different stress: Designers can make significant income from their wholesale clients, but they must spend long hours in their studios in order to fill the large orders by their clients' deadlines.

DeBaecke explains that at wholesale shows jewelry designers arrive with little inventory, since show buyers tend to purchase items by reviewing the designer's catalogue and photos of their product lines: "Buyers come to the market to put in an order, so you don't have to have extras; you'll go back to your studio to make what they want. You sell it to them for a wholesale price, which is half of what they'll sale it for. You're not making as much money per piece, but you know how much you're going to make that year. With retail, it's a crapshoot."[24]

Jewelry designers producing high volumes of inventory rely on full- or part-time staff to help them meet deadlines. Still, the constant manufacturing sometimes causes burnout for the designer. After twelve years of designing, DeBaecke had three workers and 250 wholesale client accounts across the country when she decided the work was no longer fun: "I had no time left over for anything but getting this stuff out the door. My family was suffering, my relationship with my husband was suffering. It got to be where I was working eighty hours a week. I lost the sense of play that all artists have to have."[25]

Safety Concerns

Besides being mindful of burnout and on-the-job stress, jewelry designers must be diligent in adhering to safe work practices. Their labs must provide ample ventilation, light, and ergonomic work spaces. Designers are careful in considering protective gear, such as safety glasses, ventilators, aprons, and venting systems, to shield them from the health risks associated with soldering and chemical use. Adequate lighting is also important to prevent eyestrain, as is frequently washing their hands to remove residues picked up during procedures in which they cannot wear protective gloves.

Though the industry's appreciation of these safety precautions continues to grow, DeBaecke admits that when she began designing jewelry nearly twenty years ago she was not taught to think of her safety. She now has a vascular disease of the eyes, ears, and nose, which she attributes to not being faithful about using her respirator, not utilizing a venting system, and getting physically overworked. Her current studio, which opens to the fresh air of her garden, is much better: "Now I have a HEPA filter system, a ventilation hood for the dust, and a better respirator. I also don't work as hard. When you're working twelve to fourteen hours a day, it's not good."[26] Likewise, Rosenthal, keeping in mind that metalsmiths historically have lived shorter lives, uses a respirator and venting system, and schedules a yearly physical that includes a lung exam.

Income

A shock for some designers is that purchasing this safety equipment can quickly eat into profits. Pricing their art higher is one way to ensure that their sales enable them to recoup those costs. To determine how much to charge for each piece, the designers typically figure out how long it took to design and create the piece, including material costs and labor, and then factor in how much profit they want to make per hour. Expenses outside their studios—such as gas, safety equipment, supplies, marketing fees,

Tools of the Trade

Jewelry designers utilize a wealth of tools to create their art. In broad categories, they use hand tools, including hammers, pliers, tweezers, and chisels; chemicals such as solder (an alloy usually made of lead and tin that when melted allows two metal surfaces to attach to each other), flux (a paste that when brushed on the metals allows solder to flow), and antiflux (which prevents solder from moving beyond specific areas); and adhesives such as craft cement, which offers a permanent bond and is transparent when dry, and waxes that temporarily hold jewels in place until the artist is ready to permanently attach them. Designers also use cleaning tools such as polishing cloths, buffing machines, and ultrasonic machines to make their pieces gleam and sparkle in preparation for display and sale. Jewelry designers use these tools as they see fit, in order to design and produce the most professional, eye-catching pieces they can.

and show fees—have to be figured in as well. Kummli's equation is to double her material costs, add in her hourly rate, and add an additional 25 percent for overhead expenses.

How much income a designer makes is also affected by whether the pieces sell at wholesale or retail prices, and whether the designer must pay a percentage to a sales representative or gallery in exchange for displaying and promoting the jewelry. Sales reps typically charge a commission equal to 20 or 25 percent of the value of the piece sold. Jewelry designers often loan pieces to galleries and museums on consignment for a specified amount of time, in hopes that the pieces will sell. In the process, however, designers typically lose 40 percent of the sales price, and cannot ask for the pieces back, to sell on their own, until after the specified time period. Though she makes less than when selling her pieces herself, Rosenthal has found it worth her while to place pieces in her local art museum's gift shop, where she has gained a local following.

Overall, jewelry designers can earn significant salaries, based on their marketing and manufacturing skills. The sky is the limit,

A designer uses a blowpipe to shape gold pieces. Designers use a variety of tools to create the most aesthetically pleasing jewelry possible.

says one designer who now makes more than $100,000 a year. Earnings such as this are rare, however, so many supplement their income by giving lectures or teaching workshops.

Success

For many designers, the thrill and satisfaction of following their dream often means more than riches. Working from her house in the Colorado Rockies, Kummli says that jewelry design has enabled her to follow her heart:

I remember as a kid making jewelry out of pinecones and other found objects. I was always an artist; it was the only thing I got A's in at school. I never made it to college—and with no regrets. I taught myself beadwork with books, which are my best teachers. My studio is upstairs in the family room, so I feel like I'm with my family when working. I look out a huge window that faces the Indian Peaks. This gives me inspiration and a reminder of what I'm working for: freedom and independence. It takes a long time to build a business. The money isn't always the greatest, but money isn't everything. We all have to work for a living, so why not have it be something you really enjoy? Follow your heart, work hard, and you'll succeed.[27]

True artisans are fueled by the passion for their craft. DeBaecke adds: "You're in total control of this medium with a seven-thousand-year history, something that certainly hasn't changed in five hundred years. When you finish at the end of the day, you'll have something that lasts longer than you do. You're making people happy from the get-go; it's a very happy feeling. Once you get into your groove, your work will blossom."[28]

Rosenthal adds that, to her, "success" is discovering what about jewelry design interests her and then following that path—even when potential customers end up not sharing the same enthusiasm. She explains: "For me, success is making what I want to make, having a market for it, and having people pay me a decent rate for the work I've done. If you have a piece that's not selling, it means you haven't found your market, or there is no market. I've found that it's often waiting for the right person to come along."[29]

Chapter 3

Art Therapists

Art therapy, which began to emerge in the United States in the 1930s, is a healing technique that blends art and psychotherapy. By encouraging their patients to create visual imagery through art projects such as drawing or making collages, art therapists help their patients to release powerful emotions, recover from traumatic experiences, and ultimately solve issues that stand as roadblocks to their living productive lives.

Psychiatrist Sigmund Freud, considered to be the founder of modern psychology, can be credited, in part, with the development of art therapy. Freud recognized that people often bury their emotional responses to painful experiences deep within their subconscious minds. And early art educators, in addition to observant psychologists and psychiatrists, began to notice that through the manipulation of a crayon, paintbrush, or lump of clay, patients dealing with mental and physical disorders were able to express suppressed thoughts and emotions through their art. As they did so, the patients played an important role in their own healing; in effect, they provided the road map to successful treatment. Through their art, the patients themselves brought to the surface the issues that needed to be addressed for their recovery.

Writer Mark Salmon explains how art therapy plays a detective's role in identifying the problems a person may need to resolve in order to facilitate healing:

> Imagine, for example, a young child bothered by problems in her family. When asked about why she is unhappy, she may not be able to identify the source of her feelings. But when asked to draw a picture of her family, she may unintentionally leave one of her parents out of the drawing. This may provide a diagnostic clue that the difficulty lies with that parent. The drawing that springs from a deep and spontaneous source in her mind may allow her repressed

feelings to be unintentionally revealed through the images she has produced.[30]

Helping People Cope

Because art therapy is an effective internal discovery tool, it is also helpful for healthy people who want to get more in touch with their emotions. For example, many people struggle to find the words to express the thoughts and emotions swirling through their minds. When creating artistic images in their therapy sessions, patients are able to express themselves without having to follow the strict rules of grammar and syntax demanded by oral language. And patients who cannot speak, due to an illness or physical condition, find art therapy a useful outlet for communicating their fears and needs.

Art therapy is increasingly being used to help people cope with the physical stresses that accompany many medical diseases,

An art therapist conducts a session with World War II GIs in 1946. Art therapists help their patients to cope with issues by helping them to express themselves through art.

including cancer, AIDS, and mental illness. More specifically, art therapists help adult patients cope with having to take numerous medications and undergo uncomfortable procedures by encouraging them to express their frustration through art. The act of creating something of their own seems to help calm them. In addition, children who are frightened by hospital stays have felt less fearful after an art therapist has introduced hospital objects such as syringes and bandages into their art projects. Even retirement home residents have improved their dexterity and range of motion after manipulating a paintbrush or lump of clay during art therapy sessions.

Students interested in becoming art therapists can learn the benefits of art therapy firsthand by participating as the patient in art therapy sessions. For example, when asked to draw a happy family, they might be surprised to see that they've included a picture of a dog. They might not have realized how much they missed their childhood pet, or that they still feel grief over losing that pet, until they drew the picture. Seeking out this experience gives students the confidence to know that it will help their patients. Libby Schmanke, an art therapist and substance abuse counselor, explains: "Art therapy helps people to access their feelings. The thing that surprises me is how well it works. I'm constantly thinking, 'Wow!'"[31]

The Role of Art Therapy

Art therapists introduce a variety of art-related tools to their patients during therapy sessions, not to turn their patients into better artists but to discover which art projects will best help each patient to achieve self-awareness and self-expression. Art therapist Milissa Hicks explains that art therapy is not simply an exercise in arts and crafts; it is an opportunity for a person to feel emotion as he or she makes the art:

> We emphasize the process and not the product. Everybody has the potential to make beautiful art, but we may have to teach them how to use the materials. One resident said to me, "Before you came here we thought we were just making scribbles but you taught us that we were making art." The important thing is to be open and honest in the art making process.[32]

Art students like this woman who are interested in becoming art therapists learn about the profession firsthand by participating as patients in therapy sessions.

For the art projects to be most effective, art therapists must first establish supportive relationships with patients that are based on trust. Therapists earn this trust by allowing their patients to share with them whenever they feel comfortable, without pressuring the patients. Therapists also reassure their patients that they are working in their best interests. Schmanke shares how she helps her patients feel at ease during art therapy sessions: "I tell them that I'm not going to judge what they draw. I first ask them to describe the picture. I may ask them to give it a title; sometimes I ask them to create a story about it."[33]

In general, children respond best to art therapy; to them, it is a form of play. Teenagers can be initially resistant when asked to draw, but usually discover that art therapy allows them to reveal themselves at their own pace. Adults also can be hesitant to participate, as they may be convinced that they lack artistic ability. The challenge for an art therapist, then, is to find art activities that build the confidence of his or her patient.

After learning to trust their art therapists, patients often discover that the therapy sessions provide them with a nonjudgmental place in which to vent strong feelings—whether they be anger, fear, pain, love, or low self-esteem. Bruce Miller, an art therapist who works with the terminally ill, shares how his patients have used art therapy to deal with these emotions: "I have seen people paint pictures depicting their own funeral, perhaps as a way of mourning for themselves and therefore seemingly working towards an acceptance of death, and combining this with images of their anger, clenched fists, and screaming heads, etc."[34]

Susan Heisler, author of the book *Anthology of a Crazy Lady*, explains how art therapy has helped her to deal with the depression she has experienced since childhood:

As I approached middle age and my anxiety levels began to climb, I discovered that "doodling" would gradually lessen its intensity. My original drawings were dark and grotesque, but as time went on and my healing progressed, they became freer and more whimsical. During one hospitalization, I met an art therapist who encouraged me to draw what was in my head. Up to that time, I was unable to adequately express my thoughts and feelings. I began this adventure with very primitive drawings. At first, it was difficult to identify a thought or feeling to put on paper because I had never really acknowledged my true feelings. After struggling for several months, I began drawing just to ease anxiety but was able to recognize my feelings in the pictures.[35]

Art therapists encourage their patients to study the artistic images they create, allowing them to discover their meaning. And as patients do so, they are often surprised to find that their drawings depict issues that they did not realize were bothering them. Bob Ault, who has received numerous awards for his work as a pioneer in art therapy, offers an example of how a therapy session helped two patients understand that the reason they were not as close as they used to be was because both preferred being in charge of the relationship: "I asked a married couple having marital problems to create a picture of them doing something together. They drew their tennis court. I asked if they'd forgotten something and they said, 'Oh, we forgot to draw ourselves!' Then they both drew themselves serving. It was helpful for them to be able to create a picture of themselves."[36]

Likewise, if a patient, for example, is adamant that he has forgiven the drunk driver whose actions put him in a wheelchair yet he continues to draw violent images, an art therapist would use those drawings to guide the patient into uncovering their meaning. It might be that the patient still has not yet come to terms with his anger.

Working Environments

Currently, art therapists can be found working in general hospitals, psychiatric hospitals, retirement centers, schools, nursing homes, halfway houses, and prisons. More-experienced therapists, typically those with at least five years in the field, may even choose to open private practices. But wherever they work, art therapists focus on helping patients work through problems such as eating disorders, sexual abuse, drug or alcohol addictions, relationship problems, mood disorders, or fears of an impending death.

In a school environment, an art therapist might work with students who are disruptive in class, who are deemed to have low self-esteem, or who are experiencing a painful disruption within their families, such as divorce or the death of a parent. As in their regular classrooms, the students participating in art therapy sessions are given ground rules for expected behavior. Therapist Diane Weller describes a typical first encounter with a student:

When the therapist meets the child, she introduces him to herself, the room, the materials, and the boundaries and basic limitations. Boundaries such as meeting at the same time each week for about an hour, not physically damaging the therapist, the room, or the furniture within could be stated. Within these boundaries and limitations, the child

An art therapist works with mentally challenged adults. Art therapists work in many different settings, including retirement homes, psychiatric hospitals, and prisons.

is free to use the materials as he likes. The therapist avoids praising or criticizing the work but encourages without judging its technical merit or aesthetic value. The way that the child relates to the therapist tells her much about his habitual way of relating to adults and to boundaries and limitations.[37]

In a prison, meanwhile, an art therapist might work with individual prisoners who seem incapable of interacting calmly with others. The therapist helps them understand what is triggering their anger. As a result of art therapy sessions, some prisons have significantly reduced their incidences of inmate violence.

What a Session Might Include

Therapists working one-on-one with a patient give that patient their full attention, but in group sessions, which may range in size from two to fifteen patients, the art therapist focuses on achieving a group goal. While observing individual behavior during a group session, the therapist encourages all of the participants to contribute. In a prison, for instance, an art therapist might interact with a group of inmates. While the prisoners work together on a group art project, such as a mural for the cafeteria walls, they begin to listen to and understand each other's viewpoints. This enables them to create more positive relationships outside of the therapy sessions. Another session scenario might involve a therapist working with an extended family who have expressed the desire to rebuild their relationships with each other. Fran Belvin, an art therapist in private practice in Lexington, Kentucky, shares an example of another possible scenario for a group of people who have been using alcohol to repress their feelings:

> For a group of adolescents recovering from alcohol abuse, the goal might be to express their feelings rather than deaden their feelings. The therapist might ask them to describe anger: How does anger look? What color is it? Each individual would select their own colors and shapes. But they reflect off each other; they see parts of themselves in others. The incredible thing about groups is that people get to see how others are struggling with the same issues they are. The group allows them to connect with and learn to get along with others.[38]

To get participants involved in the art process, an art therapist selects from a variety of art materials, including pastels, pencils, markers, paint, collage items, clay, and papers. The age, physical ability, or specific psychological needs of a patient may determine which art materials are used. Small children, for example, do not have the dexterity to make collages, and most adults would be frustrated by being asked to use stubby children's crayons to complete a drawing. Likewise, patients with attention disorders may become overwhelmed if provided with too many colors to choose from, or a project that involves too many steps.

Janis Spitzer, an art therapist living in Florida, is in charge of a weekly session for a small class of male high school students who are severely emotionally disabled and have varying skills in art. Spitzer explains how she stays focused on both limitations as she plans for the sessions:

> When I work with a class like this, my general goals are to enable them to produce successful works of art, gain personal

Art Therapy at Menninger Clinic

The Menninger Clinic is a world-famous psychiatric facility that was opened in Topeka, Kansas, in 1925 by three brothers, C.F., Karl, and Will Menninger. Art therapy is one of the many tools the clinic's treatment teams use to help people function better mentally, physically, and socially. The clinic tailors art therapy sessions to meet the needs of individual patients, using three types of art therapy interventions: person oriented, process oriented, and product oriented. These interventions are designed to help patients improve their cognitive skills, improve their relationship-building skills, or work through depression.

In person-oriented sessions, patients are encouraged to express themselves through art to discover repressed thoughts and feelings. The goal is to help the patients identify any underlying issues that are blocking their recovery.

In process-oriented sessions, the art therapists design activities that encourage patients to learn a new skill or change behavior. For instance, just the act of handling a new tool, such as a paintbrush, may help patients be more comfortable with experiencing new tactile sensations.

Art therapy sessions that are product oriented introduce art activities designed to give patients the opportunity to play, to use art as a creative outlet. As patients create works of art, they build feelings of pride and self-esteem.

The Menninger Clinic was the first clinic in the United States to view mental illness as treatable. Through art therapy sessions, patients can actively work toward their own healing.

insight through their artwork, and express their feelings in appropriate ways. Because these students are easily frustrated and have many challenges in their lives, it is important to plan for their success. With this in mind, I plan art activities that I hope are foolproof. I also try to use the art process as a structured means of visually expressing feelings and working through personal problems. This approach to art therapy maintains the rigid structure of the SED [State

Education Department] classroom (thus maintaining appropriate behavior, hopefully), and at the same time allows for personal expression and creativity.[39]

Traits Needed

Because of the intimate nature of their work, art therapists tend to be attentive listeners, keen observers, and have the ability to develop a strong rapport with people. They also possess empathy, flexibility, and a sense of humor, as well as good verbal and presentation skills. Belvin adds that a belief in the healing power of art is key, while Ault asserts that the desire to help people overcome pain is the art therapist's primary aim. He explains how his desire to help people is fueled by love:

> I think the concept of love in your life is very important. Dr. Karl Menninger [who opened Menninger Clinic, a world-famous psychiatric facility] states, "Love heals, both those who give it and those who receive it." I've been doing art therapy for more than forty years now and I still love it.

Art therapists must be empathetic and have a strong sense of humor. Here, a therapist shares a lighthearted moment with a young patient.

In fact, I don't know of any art therapist who has been unhappy in his or her career.[40]

Credentials a Must

To become a professional art therapist, a student must complete a master's degree in art therapy or a degree with significant emphasis in art therapy. There are currently more than twenty-five master's programs approved by the American Art Therapy Association (AATA), the primary professional membership organization representing art therapists in the United States. Students can prepare for admission to the graduate programs by enrolling in one of the college undergraduate introductory courses and preparatory programs across the country recommended by the AATA.

Art therapists must undergo years of formalized schooling. Students are required to complete a master's degree in art therapy before entering the profession.

As part of their coursework, college students participating in art therapy programs are required to take numerous studio art classes to familiarize themselves with the variety of media they are likely to use with their patients. While art therapists do not need superior art skills, they should have a broad appreciation of art. Specifically, classes in culture studies enable them to appreciate the various spiritual and artistic ways that people have expressed themselves throughout history.

After obtaining a bachelor's degree, students enroll in graduate programs such as those offered by Emporia State University in Emporia, Kansas, or the School of the Art Institute in Chicago, Illinois. The Art Institute offers one of the oldest art therapy programs in the United States—and one of the few offered by a professional school of art and design. Students in the program gain more than nine hundred hours of clinical experience and complete at least two fieldwork placements, one working primarily with children or adolescents and the other with adults or the elderly. Applicants to the program must have completed fifteen semester-credit-hours in studio art and twelve credit-hours in psychology.

To be considered for admission to the Emporia program—which requires thirty credit-hours in art courses, including three in art education, as well as twenty-four credit-hours in psychology—applicants are required to submit a portfolio of twenty slides to demonstrate their artistic competency. Applicants also meet with faculty for personal interviews in which the students are asked to explain their interest in applying. Schmanke, a graduate of Emporia, describes the program:

> [It involves] a lot of reading, a lot of papers, and a lot of doing art as a reaction to something. The faculty were very inspiring and made you feel the magic, but it was a lot of work. The program is based in the psychology department, so it has a strong psychology emphasis. In some schools the program is part of the art school or education department, so they all have different focuses.[41]

After students obtain their graduate degree in art therapy, and complete a minimum of one thousand supervised direct client hours, they apply to the Art Therapy Credentials Board (ATCB) to become registered art therapists (ATR), which gives them the necessary credentials to work in the field. An additional title of board-certified therapist (ATR-BC) may be obtained after an art therapist successfully passes a three-hour written exam administered by the ATCB. Additional continuing education credits are required to maintain the ATR-BC distinction.

Earnings and Outlook

As a career field, art therapy is growing, in part due to recent national media attention highlighting the profession after the terrorist attacks on the World Trade Center and the Pentagon on September 11, 2001. As people tried to cope with the horror of having personally experienced the attacks or the realization that they would never again see loved ones who perished on September 11, art therapists across the nation stepped in to help. Several television programs showcased how the simple art projects the therapists introduced at schools, hospitals, and community centers helped victims of all ages to express their rage, sadness, and fear.

But according to the AATA, significant education about the field still needs to take place. Many people—including those active in the medical community—remain unfamiliar with the benefits of art therapy. A recent survey by the AATA proved, in fact, that many clinical psychologists still are not clear on what art therapy is or on how to incorporate it into their patients' treatment plans.

In their local areas, many art therapists have assumed the responsibility for educating the staff of hospitals, schools, and prisons in their communities. During their presentations, the art therapists allow their patients' art to speak for itself. As the therapists share how art projects helped individual patients, they guide their audiences in understanding that art therapy is a valuable discovery and healing tool. Schmanke shares an example of how art therapy led to a breakthrough with one of her patients: "I was working in the substance abuse program in a women's prison. We were making collages, and one woman's collage was about her traumatic rape. She had been unable to tell anyone about it for years, but being able to communicate through the images worked for her. It gave us a starting point for dealing with her anger."[42] Because it produces concrete images that illustrate patients' prob-

Art Therapy Helps Children Cope After 9-11

The terrorist attacks on the United States on September 11, 2001, were particularly hard on children. Many experienced fear, bewilderment, and sadness. Some also experienced the loss of a parent or other family member.

As a way for children to cope, art therapists and school-teachers across the country quickly encouraged children to use art projects to express their feelings. Some drew pictures of burning buildings and injured firefighters; others drew crying children and people hurling themselves from windows. According to "The Art of Healing" in *U.S. News & World Report*, Salt Lake City art therapist Cathy Malchiodi was quoted as saying that the very process of creating art "prompts children to tell more than they would if you just talked about it." Psychotherapist and art therapist Ani Buk added, "When you know you can erase something, cover something over, rip it up and throw it away, these are all kinds of small, metaphoric expressions of having control."

The therapeutic value of art therapy buoyed the children, and helped their parents connect with them. While the children were able to regain an element of control and safely express their feelings, their parents could understand what their children were experiencing.

The images were effective tools in judging the children's progress. Many of the early drawings, for example, centered on fear, while later images depicted the children's focus on hope and rebuilding, demonstrating the effectiveness of their therapy.

lems, art therapy is effective in ways that other forms of therapy are not.

Because art therapy has only recently emerged, however, some states have yet to approve, or license, it as a treatment option. While the AATA is negotiating with individual states to change this, those who live in states already offering licenses can earn much more than those who do not. Until art therapy becomes a common treatment option across the country,

An Iraqi child draws a picture at an art therapy center in Baghdad. Since Saddam Hussein was overthrown in 2003, art therapists have been free to offer their services to many Iraqis.

geographic location will continue to play a deciding role in where an art therapist can find work. In states where art therapy is not licensed, art therapists may need to be licensed as counselors. Belvin explains: "It really does matter where you live. Licensure is the key to reimbursement. In California, for example, art therapists are also licensed as family counselors, which is how they bill for their patient sessions."[43]

Income for entry-level art therapy positions is approximately $25,000, and the median income is between $28,000 and $38,000. Salaried administrators can earn between $40,000 and $60,000. Art therapists with doctoral degrees, state licensure, or who qualify in their state to conduct private practice can charge as much as $75 to $90 per hour.

Art therapists can also supplement their incomes using their art. Ault, for example, offers art lessons through his private art school. Because the profession is still finding its footing, says Ault, it is an exciting and rewarding option for students interested in making their mark: "The real beauty of this profession is that you get to create it. You're presented with a problem and told to solve it. It's a great profession for self-starters."[44]

Ault adds that a career in art therapy is more financially stable than other art careers: "You can have your career in art and make money at it. You're certainly not going to be a starving artist; you can make a very comfortable living."[45]

Chapter 4

Sculptors

Sculpture, the art of producing three-dimensional representations of realistic and abstract forms, has been an avenue of human expression since ancient times. The Egyptians memorialized their pharaohs through idealized statues and busts; the Greeks and Romans decorated temples and public buildings with sculpture. The early artisans of the United States also used sculpture to decorate homes, ships, and buildings with symbols of American freedom, such as the flag and bald eagle.

While sculptured works in plaster date as far back as 7000 B.C., contemporary sculptors use a wide variety of media for their works, including rubber, beeswax, stone, wood, clay, plastic, metals, paper, glass, and wire. As well, some sculptors choose to take advantage of technology, incorporating fiber optics, neon light, and computer software into their art. In doing so, they incorporate sound, motion, and light in a way that they hope will intrigue viewers.

Sculpture in particular demands an emotional response from those who view it. Perhaps this is because, whether one is looking at an early culture's roughly carved wooden god, a grieving Madonna realistically captured in marble, or a thirty-foot-tall doll made from wire, newspaper, paste, and pink paint, the desire to reach out and touch the forms can be nearly overwhelming. Sculpture, more so than other art forms, offers viewers a tactile experience if they are allowed to stroke, hold, or play with the sculpted pieces.

Sculpture is also a very personal experience for the artist. Whether using modeling, carving, casting, or construction techniques, sculptors share parts of themselves as they work with form and texture. Even their chosen technique can convey meaning. Some sculptors, for example, approach a rectangular block of stone and carve it away, bit by bit, until the shape they have in mind appears. Other sculptors prefer the control of building their forms, adding small amounts of clay, metal, or other material until they deem the piece finished.

Building a Niche Is Key

Sculpture requires strong artistic vision and talent. While most people have the dexterity to carve a shape from a piece of wood,

Artists have used sculpture as a mode of expression since ancient times. Pictured is an ancient Greek sculpture depicting a dramatic scene from the Trojan War.

it takes a gifted artist with unique ability to imbue that carving with so much spirit and personality that another person emotionally connects with it. This is the difference between a person who is capable of only creating a bland stick figure and the artist who is able to give the carving a facial expression that makes those who view it angry, happy, or sad. A good sculptor's images surprise and perplex viewers.

To attract attention, and to find financial success, an artist needs to differentiate himself or herself from other artists. The sculptor may choose a specialty based on his or her strengths or interests. Some artists, like found-object sculptor Leo Sewell, make us gasp in appreciation of their cleverness. Sewell takes items that others consider junk—old watches, medals, utensils, and clock parts—and creates fanciful life-size sculptures of animals such as dogs, cats, and horses. In fact, Sewell has created a humorous style that has brought him notoriety around the world. Museums, corporations, and celebrities such as actor Sylvester Stallone collect his work.

Using the items he finds while rooting through dumpsters and at garage sales and church bazaars, Sewell creates art that is both old and new. His art, in particular, appeals to people who feel strongly about recycling, thus giving him a special niche, of which he has taken full advantage. His participation in the first Earth Day, a movement organized by former Wisconsin senator Gaylord Nelson and first held in 1970, helped to position him as a found-object artist. Sewell explains how aligning his work with a global issue has brought him numerous clients: "I didn't set out to solve the world's problems with junk, but I've gotten side benefits from the ecology movement."[46] So, even people who may not have an interest in art have appreciation for Sewell's sculptures.

Likewise, Pennsylvania sculptor Clayton Bright has created a niche for his art. From clay he sculpts realistic-looking animals and people and then often casts them in bronze. To ensure he stays true to nature, he spends many hours in his studio producing grid-based drawings and scribbling notes into small notebooks. For his sculpture *Red Fox*, for example, Bright observed a friend's pet fox to understand how the surface of her coat fluffed with cold weather. His recorded impressions provide every detail

The Legacy of Shape and Form

French sculptor Auguste Rodin, who died in 1917, enjoyed immense popularity for his art during his lifetime. Though he has been dead nearly ninety years, his breathtaking works of sculpture, based on his appreciation of the Italian Renaissance sculptor Michelangelo, are still very much admired for their beauty, realism, and strength of emotion.

Rodin's use of textured surfaces, which give his works a sense of life and movement, is well represented in his piece *The Thinker*. *The Thinker* was modeled for *The Gates of Hell*, a monumental door with decorations inspired by Dante's poem, *The Divine Comedy*. Rodin created *The Thinker* as a portrayal of Dante himself, and today some consider it to be the most famous work of sculpture in the world. At least twenty-one statues have been cast from Rodin's original mold, which is displayed in Paris. Copies can be found in museums around the world, including the Norton Simon Museum in Pasadena, California, and the Rodin Museum at the Philadelphia Museum of Art.

Auguste Rodin sculpted his bronze masterpiece The Thinker *as a portrait of the medieval poet Dante.*

he needs to re-create proportions and perspectives. Even though he strives for realism, he is just as interested in giving each piece an element of mystery so that viewers will respond emotionally. He explains: "I'm an observer. I can look at something and I see the form, color, and shape of it. The image comes to me easily. But how I communicate that emotion visually takes work. If someone gets a feeling from looking at my work, I've succeeded."[47]

Sculptor David Roy strives to delight viewers with his kinetic sculptures, which incorporate well-balanced parts that move when touched or set in motion by a machine. Roy's sculptures, many of which are one-of-a-kind pieces, are now displayed in galleries and private showrooms around the world. Roy explains how he and his studio, Wood That Works, got their start:

> My wife, Marji, was studying art in college while I was studying physics. She had the original fascination with machines and had done a variety of works with a mechanical flavor. My question was, "Can you make them move?" She wasn't interested in getting that technical and moved on to other things but an idea was planted. We finished school and started life in the working world. I spent nine months as a computer programmer for an insurance company and decided that it wasn't for me. I "retired" and Wood That Works was born.[48]

Another kinetic sculptor, Bruce Gray, sets his work apart from Roy's by offering his clients musical sculpture that plays a portion of a song or corporate jingle. In his sculpture titled *Cheborgie #2*, a steel ball follows a roller-coaster track, fueled by gravity, through a loop, through three chimes, around a spiral, and through a spring tunnel.

Other sculptors, such as Joseph Wheelwright, surprise viewers with the immensity of their outdoor sculptures. He creates his pieces from natural objects such as boulders and trees. Australian-born sculptor Ron Mueck enjoys shocking audiences with his realistic, and often nude, human sculptures. Cast in silicon or fiberglass and acrylic, the sculptures appear so real they seem poised to stand up or change facial expression. Mueck's talent and creativity have been well rewarded: His *Pregnant Woman* sculpture, which

The glass sculptures of Dale Chihuly are on display in some of the world's most prestigious museums. (Pictured is his Mille Fiori, *or* Thousand Flowers.*)*

stands at over eight feet tall, was purchased by the National Gallery of Australia for $461,300.

Another highly successful niche is that of glass visionary Dale Chihuly, of Tacoma, Washington. Some of the blown-glass sculptures that he leads his studio team in creating command exorbitant prices and can be found in more than 150 major museums, including the Metropolitan Museum of Art in New York City and the Louvre Museum in Paris, France. As Chihuly enjoys leading the trend in large-scale architectural installations of art in homes and public spaces, his sculptures can also be found in venues such as the Bellagio Hotel in Las Vegas, Nevada, and the canals of Venice, Italy.

Self-Taught Versus Formal Education

Some museums exclusively collect the work of these mavericks who forge their own styles rather than that of classically trained sculptors. The American Visionary Art Museum (AVAM) in Baltimore, Maryland, for instance, showcases only self-taught artists who choose not to follow anyone else's tradition. The museum expresses its choice this way:

All of us at AVAM enjoy and respect the learning that comes from academic study or through apprenticeship to a trained artist. We dedicate AVAM exclusively, however, as a place devoted to the other path of mastery—the intuitive path of learning to listen to the small, soft voice within. We believe there is great power in not knowing what will or won't work, and we adhere to the importance of not being immersed in rule-based systems which can cloud one's vision. As in science, ignorance often gives birth to genuinely new inventions and a re-examination of what has already been dismissed. Jonathan Swift defined this kind of vision so perfectly: "Vision is the art of seeing things invisible." Discovering possibilities that others do not see is what visionaries do best.[49]

Even so, new sculptors, unsure of their niche, often prefer to undergo formalized training. They learn from other sculptors who are already successful with their art. This training can begin early. For example, high school students can participate in programs such as the "Saturday Art Experience" offered by the Academy of Art College in San Francisco. This program introduces students to a number of art-related topics during six-week sessions. In the course on sculpture, novice students learn about three-dimensional techniques and materials and explore a variety of techniques and materials, including handling plaster and water-based clay. Students also gain an introduction to tools for clay modeling, demonstrations on patinas and finishes, and clay modeling from life figures.

Another option is for students to complete an internship with an experienced sculptor. The length of the internship can vary, as can the intern's tasks. Students might help with orders or arrange media events in exchange for observing the sculptor's technique and receiving one-on-one mentoring in their studios.

Workshops offered by crafts schools such as the Penland School of Crafts, the Haystack Mountain School of Crafts, and Touchstone are another option for acquiring skills. The faculty at these schools leading the one- and two-week workshops are successful sculptors already making a living from their art. The workshops are open to those who are at least eighteen years of age, and previous training is not required to participate.

Students can also earn a bachelor of fine arts in sculpture at many universities across the country and pursue a master of fine arts if they want additional training. A recent survey by *U.S. News & World Report* cites Virginia Commonwealth University, Yale University, and the School of the Art Institute of Chicago as having the nation's top three degreed sculpture programs. Other respected academic programs can be found at Otis College of Art and Design in Los Angeles, the Massachusetts College of Art, and the Academy of Art College in San Francisco. Instructors at

A German sculptor evaluates the work of his apprentice. Many sculpture students serve internships with experienced sculptors in order to learn the craft.

A sculpture student chisels a piece to submit to her instructors as part of her portfolio.

these colleges can be quite encouraging to art students. Sewell describes his art history teacher, who helped him turn his hobby of collecting junk into a successful career: "He made art seem hip. The key, to me, is all built on the love of playing with objects. The passion led to dedication. I spent a lot of time perfecting my craft and my eye and my sources."[50]

Program Highlights

Many of these programs are competitive. When considering applications to the fine arts program, Ed Schoenberg, vice president for enrollment management at Otis College, says that faculty look for a student's passion:

How do we determine your passion? We determine it by reading your personal statement about why you want to study art and design. We look to see what kinds of steps you have taken to make art while in high school or community college. That is, if your school didn't offer any art courses or very few did you take private instruction, sign up for summer programs or make work on your own? We also look at what your teachers say about you and your passion to be an artist or designer. Finally your portfolio is also a window through which we can look at your desire to make art.[51]

In these programs, novice sculptors can choose from a wide variety of art classes. Students participating in the Fine Arts 3-D program at the Massachusetts College of Art, for example, receive technical training in mold making, foundry, woodworking, and welding, as well as instruction in fibers, glass, and metals. Students can also take courses on kinetics, computer imaging, and other innovative technologies if they have an interest in incorporating them into their art. Likewise, the Academy of Art College in San Francisco attracts students with its state-of-the-art studios in welding, bronze casting, neon, ceramics, small metal/jewelry, and figure modeling.

Similar to other art majors, most college sculpture programs require students to produce a portfolio of their best work at the completion of their sophomore year. Only those students with sufficient artistic skill are allowed to continue in the program. Most schools also require a portfolio review prior to graduation, typically in the second semester of a student's senior year. While the process is intimidating for some, it helps the students become accustomed to others evaluating their art. It also gives them added confidence in being able to explain their choice of materials, technique, and niche. Also of value to students is the opportunity to participate in campus exhibitions of their work. In doing so, students begin to gain public exposure, which is necessary in turning their art into a business that will support them.

Opportunities for Exposure

Because regular sales are critical to sculptors, they strive to generate interest in their art, setting aside time to market their work. Many who are comfortable with the Internet can make use of a personal Web site that showcases their technique, promotes their exhibits, and guides buyers to their studio and/or the galleries they have chosen to represent them. The Web sites can also be used to capture visitor names and addresses, which gives the sculptors more control in marketing directly to people who have expressed an appreciation of their art. The Internet is also an effective tool for sculptors wanting to advertise their availability for workshops, lectures, exhibitions, and commissions of their work.

Some sculptors choose to hire a gallery or sales representative to handle their sales, allowing them to dedicate more time to being in their studios. The sculptor-gallery relationship can be a win-win situation for both parties. In exchange for a commission, most galleries take the responsibility for displaying the sculptor's art, as well as promoting that art through special exhibitions to which the media and public are invited. Sadie Somerville co-owns Somerville Manning Gallery in Greenville, Delaware. Keeping her clientele in mind, she explains how she chooses which sculptors to represent:

> I look for artists who show that they are seriously pursuing their careers as full-time artists. An artist demonstrates this by building a list of gallery and museum exhibitions, awards, and collections for their artwork. I try to find sculpture of the highest quality workmanship that is right for the gallery and our clientele. I search for new artists in fine art shows and juried museum exhibitions. The relationship that a gallery and an artist forge can be very important to the artist's success if they can be partners working for similar goals. Good communication is essential to this relationship.[52]

Sewell says that although galleries take roughly half of the retail price of each sculpture sold, he is happy to use their services because he does not want to deal with clients directly. He explains: "I want to make art, not run a gallery. You look more believable when someone else represents you. The only thing I won't do is sign an exclusive agreement with a gallery."[53]

An exclusive agreement gives the gallery complete control over the marketing, sales, and advertising of an artist's work. Sculptors who want more control might choose to loan their work to a museum or art center in the hopes of attracting publicity and new commissions. Many museums appreciate the opportunity to borrow art for specified time periods, as it allows them to routinely change their displays without having to raise the funds to make purchases. DeCordova Museum and Sculpture Park in Lincoln, Massachusetts, for example, invites sculptors to loan their work to the garden for up to three years. DeCordova chooses works based on the sculptor's résumé, slides of the specific sculpture the artist would like to loan, and a brief statement that includes an estimated budget for transportation and installation. DeCordova picks up these costs and determines what to display based on aesthetics, site availability, safety and security considerations, and thematic and material balance within the park. Joseph Wheelwright's pieces met the park's requirements of being durable, resistant to high wind and freeze-and-thaw conditions of a typical New England winter, and substantial enough to discourage

Sculptor Creates Life-Size Sculptures from Scrap Metal

Lyle Estill, born in Ontario, Canada, in 1962, lives in the woods of Chatham County, North Carolina. A self-taught scrap-metal sculptor, Estill creates whimsical creatures inspired by the natural world—and the trash that inhabits it. But Estill is best known for his life-size metal chess sets, for which he gained public attention in 1996.

A father of four, Estill explains that he approaches his work from a child's perspective, and relies heavily on his children for inspiration and criticism. "I create work for the popular audience," he says online in "The Story." "The look of delight on a child's face, the extended pause of a passerby, the flash of recognition in a viewer's eye, these are the moments that bind me to sculpture."

Estill first came across a life-size wooden chess set during a trip to Uppsala, Sweden. While wandering through a public park, he and his wife came upon the set and began a match. "I was inspired," he says, "and promised myself I would create one out of trash for my yard. It took me five years to scrounge enough similar materials from the woods."

Using a handheld hacksaw, an electric drill, and a passion for the project, Estill finished the chess set in August 1996. Surrounded by torches, the moon, and the stars, Estill could be found playing games on many a summer night.

"It's a surreal experience," Estill says, "sitting in your chair with your opponent pacing around in the middle of the board, listening to the owls and frogs. Sometimes a dog or cat will emerge from the darkness and walk through the game. My only regret is that I put it too close to the house. Some nights when I was lying in bed, I could see [the] torch light flickering on the ceiling, because players had shown up for a game without me."

David Berry's Sphere IV *towers over visitors to DeCordova Museum and Sculpture Park in Lincoln, Massachusetts.*

theft and vandalism. Wheelwright recently decided to exhibit ten large stone heads and three giant tree figures at DeCordova for a yearlong exhibit. More than 125,000 visitors enjoy the exhibition of large-scale, outdoor, contemporary American sculpture in the park each year, so he gained considerable exposure.

Though established sculptors can choose to develop a partnership with one or more art galleries or museums to handle most of the promotion of their art, new sculptors still building their reputations will have to do quite a bit of the legwork themselves. The Internet and e-mail now make advertising their skills much easier. The Internet is also an effective search tool for sculptors looking for information on design competitions, fellowships, and other sources of income. For instance, the New York Foundation for the Arts Source posts available grants, residencies, and apprenticeships online.

Working Environments

Artweek magazine, which considers itself the national voice of West Coast contemporary art, offers its readers information on jobs, competitions, and seminars, as well as studio space available for rent or sharing. Many sculptors need isolated work spaces—typically in studios for rent located in art centers or in spaces they carve from their homes—that allow them to focus on their art. Sewell's large Philadelphia studio affords him the space to maintain the eight hundred drawers and boxes that neatly house his found objects until he needs them. In contrast, Bright's small studio, which is perched on a steep hill overlooking his farmhouse, gives him the atmosphere he needs to be creative: simple wood construction and a bank of windows lining one wall that invites plenty of light.

African art sculptor Thaddeus Mosley also works from his home. In the basement studio of his Pittsburgh home, he carves his large sculptures, from logs felled from native western Pennsylvania

Sculpture Goes Digital

Many sculptors have begun using computer software programs to help them flesh out the designs for their artwork. Software, such as the FreeForm modeling system, enables sculptors and other artists to quickly work through design ideas using three-dimensional online sculpting. FreeForm is unique in that it is the first tool that enables sculptors and other designers to use their sense of touch while modeling on the computer.

The technology is as intuitive and expressive as physical modeling with clay or foam yet offers the productivity advantages of digital technology. Sculptors can quickly manipulate designs online to see if they work before trying them in their studios, thus reducing the waste of materials and time.

It took Michelangelo three years of chipping away at a nineteen-foot block of marble to fashion his now-famous sculpture *David*. If he had had access to computer software, Michelangelo would have been able to quickly see how his statue would look before starting with that first chip.

A Cambodian sculptor carves an image of the Buddha in his outdoor studio. Some sculptors are fortunate enough to have such a private workspace.

woods. As he finishes each piece, Mosley moves the sculptures to one of the upper rooms of his row house. He says surrounding himself with his art gives him the motivation to keep working: "I never had a house where I really liked the interior. So now I don't have to look at the interior, because I have stuff everywhere, and that catches my eye rather than the cracks in the plaster."[54]

Earnings and Outlook

Most sculptors agree that sculpture can be a very satisfying career. Fame and fortune are attainable, but it must be stressed that earnings for sculptors are unpredictable. Sculptors may have to ease into a full-time sculpting career, at first supplementing their income by teaching or working in jobs unrelated to art until they gain a reputation and loyal clients.

In rare cases, sculptures, such as Sewell's pieces, command as much as $50,000. However, Sewell, who holds a degree in economics, suggests that students considering a career in sculpture gain additional education and skills to fall back on if their art does not allow them to meet their expenses: "Even if students feel they have talent, inspiration, and dedication, it's a very dangerous field. The success rate is not high. Maybe students should have an explicit plan that by a certain date they rearrange their priorities. I only quit other work when I got busy with my art."[55]

Likewise, Bright, a former stockbroker, encourages students to have a backup plan and a timetable as they follow their creative dreams. He says, "I gave myself five years to see if I could make a living at sculpture. If I couldn't, I'd get a job. I'm pleased to say I have not had a job since 1976."[56]

Chapter 5

Graphic Designers

Graphic designers use visual elements to communicate ideas. Through designing dynamic packaging and advertisements, they help their clients influence consumer preferences and purchases. In doing so, graphic designers have a huge impact on society. The American Institute of Graphic Arts (AIGA) explains: "From humble things like gum wrappers to huge things like billboards to the T-shirt you're wearing, graphic design informs, persuades, organizes, stimulates, locates, identifies, attracts attention, and provides pleasure."[57]

Many consumers, harried from abundant choices and lack of time, often make quick buying decisions based on a product's visual appearance. Many times they choose a product because its packaging or television ads suggest that using it is exciting, fun, different, or will guarantee amazing results. Even the inexpensive disposable razor is now packaged in bright colors and with snazzy text. A graphic designer's challenge, then, is to design packaging or print or television advertisements that trigger an emotional response by consumers—and put their client's product or ideas in the forefront. Women's magazines do this; they rely heavily on their covers to capture readers. Though the magazines may all feature similar stories on relationships and staying fit, each uses bold type, color, and exciting cover photos to grab consumers' attention.

Graphic designers have a strong desire to fashion and create things, to give physical form to abstract ideas. Many, as children, preferred doodling to other activities. In addition, graphic designers enjoy translating their ideas to the world. Sheila Levrant de Brettville, a professor of graphic design at Yale University and owner of the Sheila Studio, explains her need to create visual messages this way:

> I need to make things that connect in a meaningful, useful, evocative way to others, and I like to indulge in the sensuousness of the material world. I learned that I could use design not only to reach into myself and express my own feelings, but also to reach out to others with images and words that are well researched and thought out, condensed, and transformed into a communication that could involve everyday folks in our shared public environment.[58]

Though each develops an individual artistic style, all graphic designers must meet specific standards for those working in the field. AIGA suggests that practitioners be competent in solving

Graphic designers create arresting visual imagery, such as magazine covers, to stimulate consumer interest in products.

communication problems, skilled at gathering information and generating solutions, and able to evaluate possible outcomes of these solutions.

Since designers communicate using images, they must have considerable skill in the visual arts, including a firm grasp of visual organization and composition, symbolic representation, typography, and aesthetics.

Technology's Role

Designers often combine their artistic creativity with computer technology to package messages for their clients, such as a quirky television commercial for Old Navy, a flashy Web site for Nike, the box graphics for Gateway computers, the decals for Birdhouse skateboards, or the animation for the latest Sierra game. As technology increases, graphic designers must embrace it and be comfortable with using computer software programs. Some of the most common programs used by designers are QuarkXPress, Adobe Illustrator, and Adobe Photoshop, which offer drawing, offset printing, photography, and interactive media assistance.

Computers have been around since the 1940s, but they did not become effective tools for designers until the first Macintoshes came out in 1984. Since then, technology has advanced rapidly, providing a wide range of visual elements—images, text, background textures, sounds, colors, and animated objects—that are easily manipulated, saving graphic designers and their customers time and money. Numerous ideas can be tried out on a computer within minutes, as compared to the many hours it would take to experiment using traditional paper and pen. In addition, clients can see computer "comps," or layouts, of a potential design, which gives them added flexibility in making revisions before the design is finalized. There is a downside to the technology for the designer, however: A designer must stay current with the frequent upgrades to the software programs.

While computer design tools allow designers to significantly stretch their natural abilities, designers who are interested in making a name for themselves cannot rely solely on these tools. Kathleen Marinaccio, co-owner of Fishbrain Graphic Design and a computer graphics professor at Otis Evening College in Los Angeles, teaches her students that they must be able to think cre-

Graphic designers use cutting-edge computer software to translate their artistic talents into media that appeal to consumers.

atively and draw from well-developed skill. As she introduces them to QuarkXPress, one of the most popular professional design tools on the market, she explains that proficient computer skills will not be able to mask a lack of natural ability: "QuarkXPress is so amazing, it allows you to combine all of your design elements together in one program to create a final piece of artwork. But the computer is only a tool; you must have the creative beginnings of graphic design. Otherwise, it's like handing someone a hammer and chisel without them knowing what to do with it."[59]

Responding to Client Needs

In every project, designers aim to creatively communicate their client's message. Above all, graphic design is about communication. Margo Goody, a senior designer at a publishing company, adds, "You have to respect the client and find the balance of achieving what the client wants while being articulate and selling concepts. Graphic design is about information; it's not just making pretty pictures."[60]

Designers listen to a client's needs, ponder the information, and then come up with a number of design options that mirror back what they think the client hopes to express. Much of a graphic designer's time, in fact, is spent on getting to know his or her client's business needs, work practices, values, and visual preferences. For example, a designer who learns that a particular client tends to be conservative, most likely would not suggest the use of neon colors or hip fonts in their brochures, annual report, or advertising. Only after having gained a clear understanding of the client's communications needs does a graphic designer head to the sketch pad, and eventually the computer, to produce a number of design solutions. During a typical week, the five full-time designers at Peterson and Company might create an ad campaign, one or two logos, a corporate brochure, and an alumni magazine. Bryan Peterson, who opened the Dallas-based

A team of designers brainstorms to come up with design ideas that best meet their client's needs.

design firm eighteen years ago, outlines the basic design process for any project:

> As designers we think for a living; we happen to be good at making an idea look good. In working with a client we must discover the need, define the strategy, design the piece, and then deliver the product by executing the idea properly using the right paper, the right illustrator or photographer, the right typeface, and the right color.[61]

Though Peterson only hires designers with exceptional artistic skills, he explains that those skills rank second to great people skills: "I had a great designer working for me, but he would intimidate the clients and be condescending. I'd get calls from clients saying they liked the piece, but they were moving their account to another firm because they couldn't go through that again."[62]

Theo Stephan Williams, founder of Real Art Design Group Inc. in Dayton, Ohio, adds that a healthy ego, and by that she means the maturity to value the client's preferences above the designer's own opinions, is a definite must in finding career success:

> There is nothing worse than creative types whose egos will not allow them to see the reality of a situation. If you find yourself feeling attacked by many of your peers and clients, if you find yourself wondering why no one agrees with you, if you find yourself not getting the projects that you have aspired to, take a good hard look at your ego. You will probably find that it needs an adjustment.[63]

Likewise, graphic designers must be able to graciously handle rejection of their ideas. Design is subjective, so their sense of what is interesting and appealing might vary from their clients'. Being able to let go of an idea they love in order to go with an idea the client likes better is part of being a good designer. Goody describes the fine line that designers walk during the design process: "There are times when the client can be really wrong. And there are some designers who feel really strongly about their work. You have to find a happy medium, but you have to remember that you work for the client."[64]

Design Software

Kathleen Marinaccio, co-owner of Fishbrain Graphic Design, prefers to use QuarkXpress, a design software, because of its useful features. One feature gathers all the materials for a particular design and places them in a single computer file, while creating subfiles for fonts and images. In an interview, Marinaccio explains how the software gives her complete control over projects right up to the print stage:

QuarkXpress is the greatest little program. It allows me to take various elements from clients, such as text typed in Microsoft Word and logos created in Adobe Illustrator, and combine them with my sketches I've created in Quark to create a brochure. To pull everything together I open a new file and build the front of a brochure on one page and build the back of the brochure on another page. I then import the text and logo. The wonderful thing is that I can print this out or make a PDF [portable document format] file and e-mail it to the client for his review. The client makes changes on the PDF or via e-mail and then I make the revisions in Quark. The collect-for-output feature allows me to pull everything together for the printer in that file.

The Many Faces of Graphic Design

For someone who possesses these traits, graphic design is an appealing career in that it offers numerous avenues for creative expression. Designers can choose to focus on traditional print media, such as designing the covers and inside text for books and magazines or the layout of a company's monthly newsletter. They may also create the film titles or special effects for the latest Hollywood blockbuster, the packaging for a rock group's CD, the signage and images for a museum's special exhibit on killer bees, or the signage for an arena or amusement park. It is this diversity that continues to attract Fred Showker, a graphic designer with more than thirty years' experience. He explains:

Through more than 7,000 design projects in our client billing system I've seen just about everything—from quarter-million dollar trade show booths to fifty-cent bumper stickers—I've touched on them all. I've designed more than 500 logos and literally hundreds of business start-up kits from the corner bar to Fortune 500 corporations. The design field can present just about any kind of project you can imagine, from a sand-blasted store-front concept, to anniversary books for Uncle Bob and Aunt Alice—and yes, now web sites and web pages.[65]

A Degree Matters

For these reasons, graphic design is a popular career choice. As a result, competition for jobs can be fierce, especially among the new designers entering the field each year. And while there are many design jobs in a good economy, companies typically try to handle their own design needs when budgets are tight. Education and experience are strong factors that will determine which jobs are open to a designer. Individuals rarely become graphic designers without formal training from an accredited university or art school. Both environments allow students to immerse themselves in the exploration of culture, language, words, and imagery— while also providing them with opportunities for unlimited creative freedom via hands-on projects designed to develop their artistic and communication skills.

There are currently hundreds of university programs, and numerous art schools, across the United States offering bachelors degrees in graphic design. Students interested in programs that offer the most design courses typically find them in art schools such as the Pratt Institute or the Massachusetts College of Art. Many graduates choose additional training in the form of a master of fine arts in order to better compete for jobs, particularly in a weakened economy.

Design programs vary significantly from school to school. Eva Roberts, a graphic design professor at East Carolina University's School of Art, explains that in choosing a school, students need to first determine their career goals:

I find that many high school students are not informed about the field. The industry is now dominated by computer skills, but we try to get the kids to understand that they're not software junkies but designers who use computers. Some kids come to us because they enjoy the computer and think that is reason enough to go into design. In choosing their school, students need to look at how a specific program will meet their needs. They need to look at the size of the school, the setting, and geography. Where do they want to end up working? If it's California, perhaps they should choose a school in California so that they can go ahead and become part of that community.[66]

AIGA has a comprehensive Web site filled with extensive guidance on choosing a career in graphic design. In particular, AIGA stresses the importance of students' selecting degree programs with classes built around numerous hands-on projects. These projects are critical in helping students master communication and design principles. They are also used as work samples in a student's portfolio.

A Portfolio Is Key

Colleges use portfolios to determine which students have design ability. Instructors in the graphic design programs typically review student portfolios at the conclusion of the student's sophomore year. Only those with obvious skill are allowed to continue in the program. Roberts says this policy serves to ensure that the students do not waste their time and money by continuing in a program for which they are not well suited. She explains how the process works at East Carolina University:

We try to be really tough on the students about everything. Design is a very detail-oriented business, so there has to be a lot of attention to craft—adhesives can't be bubbling up, mats must be cut straight. The students have to be able to develop a dialogue to talk about their work. I constantly challenge them to explain why they like something. Just because they like the color isn't enough; it must tie in to the concept somehow. It's important that they be able to discuss their solutions in terms of the choices made to solve a problem.[67]

During the review, ten teachers from the design department look at an average of forty portfolios. They reach a group con-

Education is key to a successful career in graphic design. Here, a group of high school students in Virginia learns the basics of design.

sensus on each, aided by several "process books" that students are required to put together to document their design processes. Students displaying an understanding of design concepts and the ability to produce several design ideas for each problem are select-ed to continue in the design program.

Roberts adds that many regional schools, such as East Carolina University, can offer an education equivalent to those of nationally recognized schools:

> [Students] might have more opportunity for outside lec-tures or nonclassroom experiences that we can't offer, but I don't think that means they are guaranteed a better educa-tion. Your degree will not get you a job; it's your portfolio that gets you the job. There are companies that won't look at you if you don't have a MFA from Yale—but the MFA from Yale won't get you the job without the portfolio.[68]

After designers graduate, a professional portfolio that contains at least ten and no more than twenty solid samples of their best work becomes their best sales tool. Potential employers, such as design firms, advertising agencies, or a company's marketing department, will scan the portfolios to evaluate whether applicants have the skills they require to meet the needs of their clients. Peterson admits that, by looking at just three samples, he can quickly determine whether a job seeker has the level of design skill that he demands from his employees.

Prospective employers often require that portfolios be dropped off prior to an interview so that they can select a hand-

How Designers Work

Exactly how do designers come up with their ideas? Brainstorming is a big part of the equation, but designer Bryan Peterson says that the process starts in the exploratory conversations designers have with their clients. Peterson describes the process he uses as the "Four D's." They stand for four stages he labels "Discover," "Define," "Design," and "Deliver."

In the discover stage, designers "download" as much information from their clients as possible. By asking exploratory questions, the designers help their clients figure out what they really need. "If clients come to a meeting saying they want a brochure," says Peterson, "the designer has to find out why— because a brochure may be the last thing they need. A designer must be able to ask questions and not be hesitant about suggesting alternatives that might be better."

In the define stage, the designer begins to formulate a number of possible design ideas and the strategy for implementing each of them. In the design stage, the designer presents the ideas to the clients via thumbnails, which are rough drawings. "The designer will ask the client, 'Is this what you told me? Do you think this meets your need?'" adds Peterson. After coming to an agreement over the best option, the designer enters the deliver stage, in which he or she executes the idea by choosing the most fitting paper, typefaces, color, illustrator, and printer.

ful of designers who have demonstrated the best design potential. Those chosen are typically invited to meet for a personal interview. During the interview, the hiring manager evaluates the candidate's ability to explain his design choices and his confidence in expressing himself verbally. Peterson shares the process his company uses:

> We have a drop-off policy as we usually get forty or fifty portfolios. We fly through them. We'll cull them down to five and I then invite those five people in to show it to me and often the rest of the design staff. What I'm really looking at is their personality and ability to present. They think I'm looking at the portfolio, but I've already seen it. I'm looking at them. Someone with a great personality might win over a better designer because I have to keep in mind that they're coming into our company to interact with the other designers and, more important, our clients. Attitude is the most important thing, then quality of skills, then potential profitability: Can I unleash them on clients and they'll make [the clients] want to come back?[69]

Peterson has some advice for students seeking their first design jobs. In addition to giving off an aura of confidence, they need to make sure that their portfolios adequately sell their skills:

> I've heard teachers tell students to put their best stuff last. That's wrong; put your best stuff first. I'll often only get through the first five pieces. I look for concept and ideas behind each piece, and then I look for typography and execution. The worst thing a student can do is to sit and try to explain their idea. That takes away the chance for the piece to speak for itself. And students should let the art director flip through the portfolio at their own pace; they shouldn't hold the portfolio hostage.[70]

Freelancing Versus a Payroll Job

Rather than jumping on board with design firms or advertising agencies, some graphic designers choose to work on their own as freelance designers. Freelancers may subcontract to other companies, but many prefer the challenge of finding their own clients.

Doing so gives them the most design control. Freelancing also gives them more flexibility regarding their work schedules, including shorter hours. Working for themselves, in their own studios, allows graphic designers to determine which projects they will take and how they will meet their deadlines.

Freelancing is not the best choice for designers who are just out of school, as they need time to refine their skills and build a clientele before handling the added pressures that come with running a business. Williams suggests that three years of working in the industry gives a designer just enough experience to accept the challenge of fully supporting him- or herself. Marinaccio explains why money issues can make working for oneself intimidating: "Some of my students say, 'I want to go freelance.' I say, 'Why?' You need to have ten to twelve clients to start with, because you'll end up keeping only five of them. And you have to learn to manage your money; forty percent of every check should go to a separate account for taxes."[71]

Freelance graphic designers must make many other decisions when they start their own businesses. Other managerial tasks to consider include deciding how to best market their design capabilities, negotiating contract fees, and budgeting the many decisions that need to be made when setting up an office. These decisions can range from which pieces of equipment to purchase or lease to ensuring that the work environment has good lighting and adequately addresses safety issues. Money will most likely be tight at the beginning, as designers need the funds to purchase computer equipment, software, paper, stamps, letterhead, and business cards. Since most clients do not typically visit a freelancer's office, it does not matter if the design studio is in one's home or in a commercial space. The only critical factors are operating professionally and meeting client deadlines.

The real upside of freelancing, Marinaccio adds, is having the ability to decline working with certain clients, to spend time with her young baby, and to call all the shots. Along with her partner at Fishbrain, Dana Moreshead, Marinaccio produces logos, movie-poster art, packaging, toy design, corporate videos, Web sites, custom comic books, and video game concepts. Marinaccio explains why she'd never leave the artistic freedom that freelancing affords her: "Some people thrive on the corporate life, but if

Steve Collier, a successful freelance graphic designer, created this poster for a coffee company. Collier and other designers enjoy the flexibility of working on a freelance basis.

you're creative and you get stuck in that box all you want to do is break out. Design is all I know and all I want to do. I have a passion for what I do. Dana's the same way; he'll think, sketch, and design from the wee hours of the morning until the wee hours of the night."[72]

Earning Potential

A graphic designer's salary is tied to many factors, including his or her skill, geographic location, and the robustness of the economy.

While new hires in a studio or advertising agency may earn less than $25,000, within three to five years they could be making up to $60,000 a year or higher. Through their freelance clients, Marinaccio and Moreshead made $350,000 in 2000.

Peterson stresses that recent graduates should be willing to work for less, and maintain a good attitude about successfully completing the lower-profile projects they are typically given until they build their skills:

> The earning curve starts out very flat for a long while and then it sharply upturns. New hires aren't tested until they've been with a firm for several years. If they have good design skills and good communications skills they can make

Although starting salaries for graphic designers can be low, experienced designers like this man checking his work at the printer often make a very comfortable living.

The Outer Limits

Graphic designers can enjoy fulfilling careers in the entertainment industry. Geoffrey Mandel has made a name for himself by blending his interests in technology and science fiction. His ability to create eye-catching graphics, and fine-tune them to the needs of television shows, has earned Mandel the praise of numerous large entertainment companies, including HBO, Warner Brothers, 20th Century Fox, and CBS.

Some of Mandel's accomplishments include designing all the signage, logos, uniform patches, prop paperwork, and still photographs used on the popular television show *JAG*; the design of control panels, alien languages, signs, and murals used in the *Star Trek: Voyager* series; and the design of signs, seals, murals, posters, uniform patches, and prop paperwork used in *The X-Files*. As well, he has worked with film clients and book and CD-ROM publishers, for whom he has created logos, brochures, and custom photographs.

Mandel has ensured his success in the fast-paced entertainment industry by creatively solving design problems and then providing prompt execution of those ideas. The finished products have made him famous in the design industry.

a lot. Within ten years they could be making $100,000, or if they own their own studio up to $500,000. But students need to realize that's only a select few. You have to be hitting all cylinders to get there. It's kind of a finicky business. But design is an incredible career. If there's anything I've done right, it's been finding the right niche for my profession. I almost feel guilty to be paid as well as I am to do what I do. But it's not easy; it takes a lot of determination and God-given talent.[73]

Notes

Chapter 1: Conservators

1. Ellen Riggs Tillapaugh, telephone interview with author, October 2003.

2. American Institute for Conservation of Historic and Artistic Works, "Becoming a Conservator." www.aic-faic.org.

3. Jonathan Thornton, telephone interview with author, October 2003.

4. Quoted in Blythe Camenson, *Careers in Art.* Chicago: VGM Career Horizons, 2001, p. 72.

5. Jae Mentzer, telephone interview with author, October 2003.

6. Sally Malenka, telephone interview with author, October 2003.

7. Thornton, interview.

8. Mentzer, interview.

9. Thornton, interview.

10. Malenka, interview.

11. Mentzer, interview.

12. Karen Pavelka, telephone interview with author, October 2003.

13. Thornton, interview.

14. Pavelka, interview.

15. Pavelka, interview.

16. Thornton, interview.

17. Pavelka, interview.

Chapter 2: Jewelry Designers

18. Carles Codina, *The Complete Book of Jewelry Making.* New York: Lark Books, 2000.

19. Maggi DeBaecke, telephone interview with author, November 2003.

20. Maxine Rosenthal, telephone interview with author, November 2003.

21. Rosenthal, interview.

22. Ivan Barnett, e-mail interview with author, December 2003.

23. Rosenthal, interview.

24. DeBaecke, interview.

25. DeBaecke, interview.

26. DeBaecke, interview.

27. Heidi Kummli, e-mail interview with author, November 2003.

28. DeBaecke, interview.

29. Rosenthal, interview.

Chapter 3: Art Therapists

30. Mark Salmon, *Opportunities in Visual Arts Careers*. Chicago: VGM Career Books, 2001, p. 114.

31. Libby Schmanke, telephone interview with author, December 2003.

32. Milissa Hicks, "Milissa Hicks—Art Therapist," *School Arts*, February 1998, p. 42.

33. Schmanke, interview.

34. Quoted in Tessa Dalley, ed., *Art as Therapy*. New York: Routledge, 1984, p. 133.

35. Susan L. Heisler, *Anthology of a Crazy Lady*. Newark, DE: Victoria Publishing, 2000. www.pneumadesign.com.

36. Bob Ault, telephone interview with author, December 2003.

37. Quoted in Dalley, *Art as Therapy*, pp. 9, 10.

38. Fran Belvin, telephone interview with author, December 2003.

39. Janis Spitzer, "Emotion Cube," *School Arts*, April 2001, p. 50.

40. Ault, interview.

41. Schmanke, interview.

42. Schmanke, interview.

43. Belvin, interview.

44. Ault, interview.

45. Ault, interview.

Chapter 4: Sculptors

46. Leo Sewell, telephone interview with author, November 2003.

47. Clayton Bright, interview with author, Unionville, Pennsylvania, May 2002.

48. David Roy, "About the Artist," 2001. www.woodthatworks.com.

49. American Visionary Art Museum, "Stuff Everyone Asks." www.avam.org/stuff/whatsvis.html.

50. Sewell, interview.

51. Ed Schoenberg, "How to Get into Schools of Art and Design," January 16, 2001. www.artschools.com.

52. Sadie Somerville, telephone interview with author, November 2003.

53. Sewell, interview.

54. Quoted in Kurt Shaw, "Sculptor Wins Award for Commitment, Passion for Art," *Pittsburgh Tribune-Review*, June 23, 2002. www.pittsburghlive.com.

55. Sewell, interview.

56. Bright, interview.

Chapter 5: Graphic Designers

57. American Institute of Graphic Arts, "What Is Graphic Design?" www.aiga.com.

58. Quoted in American Institute of Graphic Arts, "Designers at Work." www.aiga.com.

59. Kathleen Marinaccio, phone interview with author, November 2003.

60. Margo Goody, phone interview with author, November 2003.

61. Bryan Peterson, phone interview with author, November 2003.

62. Peterson, interview.

63. Theo Stephan Williams, *The Streetwise Guide to Freelance Design and Illustration*. Cincinnati: North Light Books, 1998, p. 19.

64. Goody, interview.

65. Quoted in Designers' Bookshelf, "Editor's Message." www.design-bookshelf.com.

66. Eva Roberts, phone interview with author, November 2003.

67. Roberts, interview.

68. Roberts, interview.

69. Peterson, interview.

70. Peterson, interview.

71. Marinaccio, interview.

72. Marinaccio, interview.

73. Peterson, interview.

Organizations to Contact

American Art Therapy Association (AATA)
1202 Allanson Rd., Mundelein, IL 60060
(888) 290-0878
www.arttherapy.org

AATA, a nonprofit organization of approximately five thousand professionals and students, believes that the creative process of making art is healing and life enhancing. It has established high standards for art therapy education, ethics, and practice.

American Institute for Conservation of Historic and Artistic Works (AIC)
1717 K St. NW, Suite 200, Washington, DC 20006
(202) 452-9545
http://aic.stanford.edu

AIC is the national membership organization of conservation professionals dedicated to preserving the art and historic artifacts of our cultural heritage for future generations.

American Institute of Graphic Arts (AIGA)
164 Fifth Ave., New York, NY 10010
(212) 807-1990
www.aiga.com

AIGA is the place where design professionals turn to exchange ideas and information, participate in critical analysis and research, and advance education and ethical practice.

Gemological Institute of America (GIA)
World Headquarters The Robert Mouawad Campus
5345 Armada Dr., Carlsbad, CA 92008
(800) 421-7250
www.gia.edu

GIA is the world's foremost nonprofit institute of gemological research and learning.

Heritage Preservation

1730 K St. NW, Suite 566, Washington, DC 20006

(202) 624-1422

www.heritagepreservation.org

Heritage Preservation provides a forum for discussion, under-standing, and awareness of national conservation and preserva-tion needs. It also offers bibliographies and other publications on a wide range of conservation and related topics.

International Sculpture Center (ISC)

14 Fairgrounds Rd., Suite B, Hamilton, NJ 08619-3447

(609) 689-1051

www.sculpture.org

ISC seeks to expand public understanding and appreciation of sculpture, and promote a supportive environment for sculpture and sculptors. Members include sculptors, collectors, patrons, ar-chitects, developers, journalists, curators, historians, critics, edu-cators, foundries, galleries, and museums.

Jewelers of America (JA)

52 Vanderbilt Ave., 19th Floor, New York, NY 10017

(800) 223-0673

www.jewelers.org

JA is the national association for retail jewelers. The Web site of-fers a listing of available training programs and schools by cate-gory and state.

National Coalition of Creative Arts Therapies Associations (NCCATA)

8455 Colesville Rd., Suite 1000, Silver Spring, MD 20910

(201) 224-9146

www.nccata.org

Founded in 1979, this group is an alliance of professional associa-tions dedicated to the advancement of the arts as a form of ther-apy. NCCATA represents more than eight thousand individual members of six associations of creative arts therapies: art, dance/movement, drama, music, poetry, and psychodrama.

National Endowment for the Arts (NEA)
1100 Pennsylvania Ave. NW, Washington, DC 20506
(202) 682-5400
http://arts.endow.gov

Established in 1965 as an independent agency of the federal government, the NEA provides national recognition and support to both new and classic works of art, thus preserving and enhancing our nation's diverse cultural heritage.

National Sculpture Society (NSS)
237 Park Ave., New York, NY 10017
(212) 764-5645
www.nationalsculpture.org

NSS promotes excellence in figurative and realist sculpture throughout the United States. A not-for-profit organization, NSS has four thousand members, including some of the world's finest sculptors, architects, art historians, conservators, and other allied professionals.

Society of American Silversmiths (SAS)
PO Box 72839, Providence, RI 02907
(401) 461-6840
www.silversmithing.com

SAS was founded in 1989 as the nation's only professional organization devoted solely to the preservation and promotion of contemporary silversmithing. Member silversmiths have been juried into SAS based on their outstanding technical skill.

Society of North American Goldsmiths (SNAG)
4513 Lincoln Ave., Suite 213, Lisle, IL 60532-1290
(630) 852-METL [6385]
www.snagmetalsmith.org

An organization for jewelers, designers, and metalsmiths created to encourage the free exchange of information, to promote the field to a wider audience, and to recognize outstanding creative achievement.

For Further Reading

Books

Blythe Camenson, *Careers in Art*. Chicago: VGM Career Horizons, 2001. Explores careers in graphic arts, fine arts, art education, museum studies, and art sales. Each chapter outlines job duties, qualifications, and career outlook, and provides interviews with working professionals.

Susan H. Haubenstock and David Joselit, *Career Opportunities in Art*. New York: Checkmark Books, 2001. A useful guide for those seeking overviews of art careers in design, education, journalism, museums, galleries, auction galleries, and art-related businesses.

Sean More, *How to Make Money as an Artist: The 7 Winning Strategies of Successful Fine Artists*. Chicago: Chicago Review Press, 2000. This how-to guide debunks the myth that artists cannot find financial success; it explains how to exhibit in shows, win awards, gain commissions, and make sales to collectors.

Mark Salmon, *Opportunities in Visual Arts Careers*. Chicago: VGM Career Books, 2001. This guide highlights careers in design companies, fine art, teaching art, art therapy, and freelance design.

Web Sites

Arts in Therapy Network (www.artsintherapy.com). An international community for creative arts therapists, including those who use art, music, play, dance, drama, poetry, and pet therapy to help others.

ConservationInfo.com (www.conservationinfo.com). Offers helpful information on art conservation as a career.

Haystack Mountain School of Crafts (www.haystack-mtn.org). Offers jewelry designers two- and three-week sessions in blacksmithing, ceramics, fibers, glass, graphics, metals, and wood.

HOW (www.howdesign.com). *HOW* is the industry's leading creativity, business, and technology magazine for graphic design professionals. Each issue provides a mix of essential business information, up-to-date technology tips, and profiles of professionals who are influencing design.

Penland School of Crafts (www.penland.org). Offers one-, two-, and eight-week workshops on books and paper, clay, drawing, glass, iron, metals, photography, printmaking, textiles, and wood.

Sculptor.org (www.sculptor.org). Contains more than four hundred pages of resources and tools and twelve thousand links. A top site for sculpture and sculptors.

Touchstone Center for Crafts (www.touchstonecrafts.com). Offers beginners and seasoned artists more than one hundred weeklong and weekend courses taught by some of North America's finest artisans.

Works Consulted

Books

Carles Codina, *The Complete Book of Jewelry Making*. New York: Lark Books, 2000. An excellent guide on jewelry techniques with accompanying photos. An added bonus is step-by-step instruction for seven projects.

Tessa Dalley, ed., *Art as Therapy*. New York: Routledge, 1984. Introduces art as a therapeutic technique.

Edith Kramer, *Art as Therapy with Children*. Chicago: Magnolia Street Publishers, 1993. This book provides a general overview of art therapy and examples of the different ways art materials are used.

Cathy Malchiodi, *The Art Therapy Sourcebook*. Los Angeles: Lowell House, 1998. Provides an overview of the field of art therapy, explaining how art is a proven tool for growth and transformation.

Tim McCreight, *Jewelry: Fundamentals of Metalsmithing*. Madison, WI: Hand Press Books, 1997. McCreight shares nearly three decades of design expertise.

Andrew Oddy, ed., *The Art of the Conservator*. Washington, DC: Smithsonian Institution Press, 1992. This is a great book for understanding the role of conservator. Eleven important works are highlighted, with a description of the unique restoration problems each presented and how they were overcome.

Elizabeth Olver, *The Art of Jewelry Design from Idea to Reality*. Cincinnati: North Light Books, 2002. An excellent resource that includes essential design tools, elements of design, and the stages of the design process. Numerous photos highlight concepts.

Daniel Schodek, *Structure in Sculpture*. Cambridge, MA: MIT Press, 1993. Sculpture students will learn much from the text and photos included in this book. Basic principles, shapes and elements, materials, and balance and structural stability are all addressed.

Elizabeth Taylor, *My Love Affairs with Jewels*. New York: Simon & Schuster, 2002. Film actress Elizabeth Taylor offers a personal tour of her jewelry collection, one of the world's foremost.

Philippe Tretiack, *Cartier*. New York: Universe Publishing, 1997. A great read about Cartier, the design house that has supplied aristocracy and millionaires with remarkably designed pieces. Numerous photos accompany the biographical information.

Theo Stephan Williams, *The Streetwise Guide to Freelance Design and Illustration*. Cincinnati: North Light Books, 1990. Written for designers and illustrators who want to be independent and who have the skills to run their own businesses, this book includes everything from pricing and marketing to negotiating and copyrighting.

Janet Zapata, *The Jewelry and Enamels of Louis Comfort Tiffany*. New York: Harry N. Abrams, 1993. The analysis of the development of Tiffany's jewelry is a must read for would-be designers.

Periodicals

Milissa Hicks, "Milissa Hicks—Art Therapist," *School Arts*, February 1998.

Janis Spitzer, "Emotion Cube," *School Arts*, April 2001.

Internet Sources

American Institute for Conservation of Historic and Artistic Works, "Becoming a Conservator." www.aic-faic.org.

American Institute of Graphic Arts, "Designers at Work." www.aiga.com.

———, "What Is Graphic Design?" www.aiga.com.

American Visionary Art Museum, "Stuff Everyone Asks." www.avam.org/stuff/whatsvis.html.

Chessworks, "The Story," http://thechessworks.com/thestory.html.

Designers' Bookshelf, "Editor's Message." www.design-bookshelf.com.

Susan L. Heisler, *Anthology of a Crazy Lady*. Newark, DE: Victoria Publishing, 2000. www.pneumadesign.com.

Robert Miller, "Art Therapists Help Patients Paint Bright New Vistas," *Dallas Morning News*, Business Day, 1997. www.art therapy.org.

David Roy, "About the Artist," 2001. www.woodthatworks.com.

Ed Schoenberg, "How to Get into Schools of Art and Design," January 16, 2001. www.artschools.com.

Kurt Shaw, "Sculptor Wins Award for Commitment, Passion for Art," *Pittsburgh Tribune-Review*, June 23, 2002. www.pittsburgh live.com.

Marianne Szegedy-Maszak, "The Art of Healing," *U.S. News & World Report*, 2004. http://www.usnews.com.

Index

Picture Credits

About the Author

Sheri Bell-Rehwoldt, who enjoys writing about creativity and uniqueness, is an award-winning freelance writer who has penned numerous articles on the arts, health, human resources, and interesting people for Web sites and national, trade, and regional publications, including *American Profile*, *Family Circle*, *HR Innovator*, and *Ladies Home Journal*. She also writes and edits for business and nonprofit clients. This is her first book for Lucent.